THE BIRDING PRO'S
FIELD GUIDES

I0126706

Birds of Vermont

Marc Parnell

Naturalist & Traveler Press

To my mother,
For whom this book was originally intended.

May all readers of this field guide
enjoy birding as much as we have together.

Printed in the United States of America
First Printing, 2022

ISBN: 978-1-954228-31-3
Library of Congress Control Number: 2021932338

Naturalist & Traveler Press
Cleveland, Ohio

www.thebirdingpro.com

TABLE OF CONTENTS

Note: All species listings are alphabetized and located in the rear index for quick reference.

HOW TO USE THIS GUIDE

Birding by Comparison

This field guide series introduces a new method to bird identification: the ***birding by comparison approach***. The objective of this technique is to empower birders to understand how birds might appear in a foreign environment before they have even observed the species, allowing them to more quickly and intelligently respond in the field.

First, close your eyes and imagine the size and silhouette of a well-known suburban species, such as the Northern Cardinal. Consider (from memory) how it perches on a branch or birdbath, how large it seems compared to the nearby leaves and vegetation, and how it appears from farther away—such as from across the street.

Now, consider the similarly sized Gray Catbird, a common bird of thickets and wooded edges. While less frequently observed by suburbanites, most nature walks in the warmer months will turn up at least several loudly *mewing* individuals. With eyes closed, superimpose the silhouette of a gray Northern Cardinal into a dense thicket, with the tail visible from one gap in the leaves and the head visible in another. Finally, consider the detailed images and behavior accounts given on the Gray Catbird species page, and modify the mental imagery accordingly.

Such visualization techniques allow the birder to transform each species into a three-dimensional, breathing creature that is practically waiting to jump from the pages. In addition, they prepare the birder in advance for how to locate and identify these birds in a simple, memorable fashion.

Male Northern Cardinal at left, Adult Gray Catbird at right.
(Note: Both the Gray Catbird and Northern Cardinal are
listed in this guide as measuring 8 ¾ in. from bill to tail.)

Locating Birds in This Guide

When sequentially flipping through the pages of this field guide, you will be viewing all common birds of the region *from largest to smallest*. Once a species in question has been narrowed to a selection of pages, the large, clearly identifiable images allow for an easy and painless identification.

In addition, consider the following reference sizes, which may prove helpful when starting out:

- **Very, Very Large**: Great Blue Heron (45 in.), Canada Goose (37 in.), Turkey Vulture (28 in.)
- **Very Large**: Mallard (23 in.), Red-tailed Hawk (22 in.), Ring-billed Gull (19 in.), American Crow (19 in.)
- **Large**: Cooper's Hawk (16 in.), Rock Dove/Pigeon (13 in.), Common Grackle (12 in.)
- **Medium-Large**: Mourning Dove (12 in.), Blue Jay (11 in.), American Robin (10 in.), Northern Cardinal (8 ¾ in.)
- **Medium**: European Starling (8 ¼ in.), Red-winged Blackbird (8 in.), Brown-headed Cowbird (7 ½ in.)
- **Small-Medium**: Downy Woodpecker (6 ¼ in.), Song Sparrow (5 ¾ in.), House Finch (5 ½ in.)
- **Small**: Chipping Sparrow (5 ½ in.), White-breasted Nuthatch (5 ¼ in.), Carolina Wren (5 ¼ in.)
- **Very Small**: American Goldfinch (5 in.), Common Yellowthroat (4 ¾ in.), Ruby-throated Hummingbird (3 ¼ in.)

All species are also listed in the rear index, which provides a complete listing of the birds covered in this field guide.

Understanding Species Listings

Each listing contains detailed information on many aspects of the species' life, sorted into a series of straightforward sections. For more detailed explanations of the written sections, consider the diagrams on the following two pages.

In addition, each species features a full page of color photographs. These have been carefully selected to highlight each species' most significant features and field marks, as well as accurately present the bird in its typical habitat. This should provide a baseline reference when first studying a particular bird, and will thus closely correspond with many field observations.

Frequency Rating: This provides a one to five rating of how likely an average birder is to see the species in a given year. Novices should mostly focus on three- to five-rated birds, while advanced birders will likely be familiar with birds of all ratings.

Common Name: This is the name most often used when describing the species.

Habitat: Describes where the species is most likely to be observed in the wild.

Wild Diet: Describes the food sources most often taken by this species (feeder diet is covered separately in *Bird Feeding Tips*, if applicable).

Migrate: This explains if, or the extent to which, a species migrates in this region.

Eggs: Describes the color, markings, length, and number of eggs. Also, lists the number of broods if greater than one.

Compare to Similar Species: Describes the significant field marks for distinguishing this bird from similar species.

Species Map: Dark-highlighted states indicate the species' presence in the state, while lighter states (of which there are none for the Mourning Dove, a widely common bird) indicate the species' relative absence from the state.

MEDIUM TO LARGE

⑤ **MOURNING DOVE.** *Ze*

SIZE: 12 in.
HABITAT: Open woods, fields, suburbs, roა
WILD DIET: Various seeds.
BEHAVIOR: Often observed perching on repeatedly *hooing* with its signature, melancl is not an overly picky eater. To accompany it swallows fine rocks or sands to aid in digestiი itself on the ground, with wings and tail splay
MIGRATE? Partially.
NESTING: Hidden among tree branches, objects such as eaves and gutters. Cup-shap grasses, and small sticks. About 8 in. across.
EGGS: White. Length of 1 in. Total of 2. Usი raise up to 6.

BIRD FEED:

FEEDER DIET: Black-oil and hulled sunflowe hearts, millet, oats, nyjer, milo. **FEEDER TY**F **BEHAVIOR:** May rest or forage beneath feedeჽ Hawks, and sometimes Sharp-shinned or even R

COMPARE TO SIMILAR SPECIES: Mჼ found in less urban areas. Tapered, feathered which are very different from the more rectა American Kestrels, not to mention many othჼ

DID YOU KNOW? Occasionally called turt in flight—reaching speeds of up to 55 mph as

J   F

BIRDS (8 ½ - 12")

٦aida macroura.

Size Category: Provides a convenient, color-coded indicator of bird size. Eight different sizes are used throughout this book, all of which are listed (with examples) on Page 5.

Size: Indicates the average length from bill to tail.

١dsides.

wires, fences, roofs, and in trees, while ١oly call. Pecks for food on the ground, and ١ voracious appetite for seeds, this species ٠n. Occasionally may be observed sunning ،ed out.

Scientific Name: This is the name most often used in academic literature.

in shrubs, on the ground, or in artificial ed, and constructed with conifer needles,

١ally raises 2-3 broods each year, but may

Behavior: This section provides an extended, in-depth description of how the species spends its days (e.g., foraging, flocking, aggression, flying style, songs and calls, etc.).

١NG TIPS

r seeds, safflower seed, cracked corn, peanut ٠ES: Ground, platforms, hoppers. **FEEDER** rs. Common prey for feeder-raiding Cooper's ٠ed-shouldered Hawks.

Nesting: Describes the location, construction, and size of this species' typical nests.

١ch paler than Rock Doves, and usually ٠ tails are easily observable when perching, ١ngular tails of Sharp-shinned Hawks and ٠r visual differences.

le doves, these birds are anything but slow ٠ they whistle through the air.

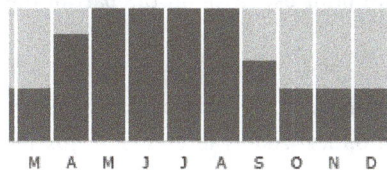

Bird Feeding Tips: For birds that visit feeders, this section describes which types of food are consumed (ordered by preference), which feeders are most often used (also ordered by preference), and a brief description of behavior.

Did You Know: Provides an interesting fun fact for each species, and often much more.

M A M J J A S O N D

Monthly Birding Forecast: Provides a simplified chart to show when the species is most observable locally. This forecast allows for birders to selectively target certain species by time of year.

INTRODUCTION TO BIRDING AND BIRD FEEDING

BIRDING

Gear Basics

First on any new birder's wish list must be a pair of suitable binoculars. These can be advertised with a dizzying array of specifications and features.

As far as lenses and magnification are concerned, an 8x42 pair is normally best for beginners and intermediates. The first number refers to the magnification, which should not exceed 10, and is ideally 7 or 8; the second number refers to the size of the objective lens (e.g., 42 mm), with smaller sizes decreasing overall brightness and field of view. If binoculars with too high of magnification are used, the effective field of view is decreased to the point that quickly locating birds can be extremely difficult.

A good pair of binoculars should cost at least $75, but no more than $300. There are many well-reviewed bins that fall squarely within this price range. However, advanced or professional birders may use binoculars which cost up to $2,500. Keep in mind that increases in cost are often accompanied by marginal benefits, and that an inexpensive pair of binoculars can provide nearly all of the same thrills for a lower entry price, especially for novice or occasional birders.

A mobile application with bird sounds is the next logical item for most birders, and several free options are widely available from most app stores.

This field guide does not include written descriptions of bird calls and songs for every species—though many are included—as it can often be difficult to fully appreciate or even understand songs in this format. Consider downloading the free Audubon (by the National Audubon Society) or Merlin (by the Cornell Lab of Ornithology) mobile apps, which provide audio tracks for each species in a given locality. In addition, some apps even identify birds by their calls in real time, but results can be inconsistent and often require prior expertise on the part of the birder.

A few optional extras must also be mentioned. Many cameras, particularly high-zoom bridge models, are now offering optical zooms in excess of 50x for prices less than $300, which likely proves the most logical starting price point. Spotting scopes are land-based, tripod-mounted telescopes specialized for observing wildlife from a distance, and particularly suited for locating distant shorebirds and waterfowl; many of these scopes can offer up to 60x optical zoom, though quality models often begin near $1,000. Finally, for longer hikes, consider purchasing a bottle of high-SPF sunscreen, a high-capacity water bottle, a first-aid kit, and wading boots (for submerged trails).

Approaching and Identifying Birds in the Field

Keep a safe distance from birds, and be wary of making any sudden movements or noises. Many species are extremely wary of humans, and can vanish into a thicket or behind a tree before the birder is even aware of their presence. (It must also be noted that actively interfering with a bird's ability to forage or nest can affect their chances of long-term survival.) Finally, only explore birding patches on public land, and do not trespass on private property without prior permission—even if there might be a life-list bird lurking in the shadows!

When identifying birds in the field, a stepwise process is often very useful, both for remembering information and prioritizing identification steps. Consider the following:

- First, consider the behavior and habitat of the bird. Is it wading in the shallows of a marsh, like a heron, or perching on the shingles of a house, like a dove?
- Estimate the size of the bird relative to that of others you have observed. For instance, is the bird approximately sparrow-sized, cardinal-sized, duck-sized, etc.?
- Determine the color and primary field marks of the bird in question. If the bird is red, medium-sized, and perched in a tree, does it have a crest like a male Northern Cardinal or black wings like a male Scarlet Tanager?
- Continue to observe the bird while considering these criteria, if possible. Viewing a bird from multiple angles, listening to its vocalizations, and observing its general behavior can further elucidate any puzzling identification challenge.

Finally, consider seeking out local Audubon societies or birding clubs. Partnering with a more experienced companion in the field is one of the best ways to double-check observations and learn more specific or situational techniques. In addition, many of these local organizations sponsor conservation and awareness efforts which are critical for the maintenance of nature for future generations.

BIRD FEEDING

Selecting Feeders

The first feeder selected should be a large, squirrel-proof tube or hopper. These are particularly easy to monitor and refill, and can be filled with a high-quality variety mix or with black-oil sunflower seeds.

For a second feeder, consider mounting suet cages on trees throughout the yard. These can be found in standardized sizes, which fit a wide variety of third-party suet cakes. Hands-on birders might also consider applying the suet directly to the tree bark: most suet cakes easily rub onto the trunk, and provide a more accessible food source for many avian visitors.

The majority of feeder setups would also benefit from a large platform, which can be hung from tree branches or fastened atop a tall, metal pole. Platforms best suit ground-feeding birds, as well as many other species which may be too large to comfortably perch at a tube or hopper feeder. The platform is best filled with a variety mix or with black-oil sunflower seeds.

As a bonus feeder, consider spreading excess seed on the ground nearby, for ground-feeding birds (e.g., doves, sparrows) and mammals (e.g., squirrels, chipmunks). This can often be the most cost-effective way to attract the most species to the backyard, though the ground must be occasionally raked to rid the area of built-up droppings or decomposing feed.

After this point, platform cups with dried mealworms, fresh fruit (e.g., oranges, grapes, or apples), or very small amounts of grape jelly can be added, as well as dedicated hummingbird feeders, hanging seed bells, ground-feeding trays, and hanging thistle tubes for finches. Careful experimentation is often a central tenet of successful bird feeding.

Squirrel-Proofing Feeders

Squirrels are immensely resourceful creatures, and are unlikely to turn down an easy meal—particularly at dedicated feeding stations, which present an enticing opportunity. To ensure that bird feeders serve their originally intended purpose (i.e., feeding the birds), consider the following potential solutions:

- Situate each feeder at least 7-8 ft. away from all nearby trees and branches
- Utilize a tall, metal pole, measuring approximately 5 ft. from the ground to the base of the feeder
- Hang feeders from a line laterally fastened to multiple trees (i.e., the clothesline method)

- Set up a dedicated ground-feeding station to divert squirrels' attention, with a platform or section of ground amply stocked with black-oil sunflower seeds and/or peanuts

Try to refrain from using cayenne pepper, or products which incorporate this spice. While partially effective in discouraging squirrels from consuming the feed (birds have far less sensitive taste buds than mammals), this can be dangerous for the squirrels; if the squirrel touches its eyes after feeding, it may attempt to desperately claw out the foreign particles, leading to partial or full blindness.

Situating Feeders

Bird feeders should be at least 8-12 in. apart from one another, providing ample room for birds to access all openings and perches, as well as reducing the stress imposed on birds when feeding in excessively close quarters.

Additionally, it must be noted that hundreds of millions of birds die each year due to window strikes. As such, best practice for situating feeders is as follows: either 25 feet or more from all nearby windows, or immediately next to any windows. The primary concern with feeders situated in the danger zone—about three to 25 feet away from windows—is that birds can generate enough momentum to make a window strike fatal, while not having sufficient time to avoid the obstacle if quickly fleeing the feeder station (e.g., from a predator, or to seek shelter).

In conclusion, situate feeders as close as possible to low shrubs and/or groves of trees: birds feel more safe with lots of nearby shelter. A metal pole can be used to support a large platform, which is often most effective for attracting the widest variety of birds. All remaining feeders should be squirrel-proofed (e.g., weight-sensitive openings, cages with narrow entrances, or thistle mesh tubes), if possible.

Maintaining Feeders

Bird feed must be replaced at least once a week, particularly in hot or rainy weather, when mold and bacteria growth can be most pernicious. In the special case of hummingbird feeders, each feeder should be completely emptied and refilled at least once every five days, and every two days in warmer weather. Otherwise, the sugar water mixture can ferment, producing toxic levels of alcohols.

THE BIRDING PRO TIP

Sugar water for hummingbirds can be made at home with a four-parts water, one-part white sugar recipe. The water must be brought to a boil before adding sugar, thoroughly stirred, and then allowed to cool afterwards.

In general, each feeder should also be taken down at least once each month for cleaning. The following steps provide a quick guide to this simple process:

- First, empty all seed.
- Second, scrub away any debris or bird droppings.
- Third, soak the feeder in a weak cleaning solution (e.g., one-part bleach to 10-parts warm water), and gently scrub with a towel.
- Finally, once completely dried (to avoid the growth of mold), the feeder can be refilled and rehung.

If feeders are not regularly cleaned, contagious diseases can quickly spread among local flocks. A commonly observed disease, bacterial conjunctivitis, is common in eastern House Finches; first observed in the 1990s, this causes avian pink eye and eventually leads to full blindness, which itself results in starvation or premature predation.

Nest Boxes and Birdbaths

When considering nest boxes, first ensure that the box in question is made of wood, rather than plastic. Furthermore, individual species often require specific sizes and designs of nest boxes. If you seek to target certain birds, consider searching online for blueprints or for well-reviewed nest boxes listed for sale. Many commercially available, decorative birdhouses fail to successfully attract breeding pairs of birds.

On another note, birdbaths tend to be a fantastic way to attract birds to any backyard. Maximum depths of ¾ to 2 ¼ in. are preferable, with shallower areas near the edges of the basin. A central bubbling feature, if present, helps to prevent insects from settling and congregating around the bath.

Birdbaths must be cleaned two to three times each week. Each basin must be completely emptied, scrubbed clean, soaked in a 1:10 bleach-to-water solution, and thoroughly rinsed before being refilled. If these tasks are not diligently completed, the birdbath can become a breeding ground for various avian diseases—defeating the original purpose of supporting local bird life.

Additional Notes

Plant as much *native* vegetation as possible, and consider leaving brush piles for birds—and other animals—to use as a source of shelter. These simple steps can drastically increase both the diversity and concentration of wildlife in the backyard.

Furthermore, if Black Bears are locally common, consider only setting out feeders in winter (i.e., when bears are hibernating). Otherwise, bears can prove to be a very dangerous nuisance: knocking down and destroying feeders, curiously investigating other parts of the backyard, and even approaching the house. Throughout the remainder of the year, use dense plantings of native shrubs and trees, as well as birdbaths and nest boxes, to safely attract avian visitors.

COLLECTED LIST OF FAQs

BEHAVIOR

Q: *Where do birds go to sleep?*

A: First of all, one common misconception must be addressed: birds do not sleep in nests, with the exception of actively incubating females. Instead, birds sleep—or roost—in a variety of other secure locations.

Waterfowl tend to sleep directly on the water, or on protected shorelines (i.e., with plenty of brush, or on islands). Often present in large flocks, ripples on the water's surface can alert the individuals to any approaching threat. Interestingly, standing waterfowl tend to favor a one-legged stance at their roosts, with the other leg tucked into the belly feathers for warmth.

Large wading birds, such as herons and egrets, tend to roost in the shallows or low in trees, depending on the species. Like some species of waterfowl, wading birds are known to frequently sleep on one leg.

Woodpeckers and nuthatches often roost in cavities, such as natural tree hollows or artificial substitutes. Some birds which nest in cavities, such as wrens, chickadees, and bluebirds, may retire to separate cavity roosts as well.

Crows, starlings, and swallows roost communally. It may be quite common for observers to notice several hundred crows or starlings settling in a grove of trees just before dusk, depending on the location. This strength-in-numbers approach increases safety by application of a collective effort to surveil for predators.

Diurnal birds of prey, such as hawks, may sleep on exposed perches (e.g., telephone poles) or tree branches. In colder weather, individuals are more likely to roost closer to the trunks of mature trees, which slowly dissipate daytime warmth throughout the night.

Finally, most other passerines (i.e., perching birds) tend to roost on sheltered perches in densely vegetated trees, bushes, thickets, and brush piles, often depending on their most frequent daytime haunts. If a predator attempts to climb tree trunks in search of a hasty meal, subtle vibrations are transmitted up the tree and warn any roosting birds of the threat. Like other birds, passerines are more likely to roost closer to the tree trunk during colder bouts of weather.

Q: *Do birds mate for life, or do they change mates throughout a single season?*

A: The vast majority of birds form a moderately stable pair bond for the breeding season, though there may be varying degrees of promiscuity (or "cheating"). The pair typically separates by the end of the summer, selecting new mates the following spring. Fewer than one-tenth of all birds exhibit non-monogamous behavior over a single breeding season, with the following patterns occasionally being observed: polygyny, wherein the male takes and protects multiple female mates (e.g., Red-winged Blackbirds); polyandry, where each female has multiple male mates (e.g., Spotted Sandpipers); and full promiscuity, where a less discernible, transient relationship between each "pair" is observed (e.g., some hummingbirds).

Q: *How smart are birds, really? And isn't the expression "bird-brain" used for a good reason?*

A: Birds are fantastically intelligent. Many corvids (e.g., ravens, crows, and jays) possess advanced problem-solving and communicational abilities surpassing those of even domestic dogs and cats, and numerous other species have been proven to have phenomenal long-term memories and multitasking abilities. Among the smartest families of birds are the parrots and the corvids.

Q: *Why don't birds sing as much in the wintertime?*

A: For many birds, the primary purposes of singing include courtship and territorial defense. However, the breeding season only extends from spring through late summer; additionally, many birds may flock together in winter to cooperatively search for scarce food sources, or even disperse over wider, undefended areas. Consequently, some species may lose the ability to sing during these colder months, while others are simply more judicious with the use of their voices.

Q: *When do birds migrate, and how long does it take?*

A: Most birds migrate north between March and May, and migrate south between late August and early October: with more senior individuals making these trips first. It may take some species up to two months to complete their journeys, while shorter-distance migrants may take less than a month. In addition, many birds (with a few exceptions, such as hawks, which soar on warm-air currents by day) take migration flights by night, touching down in a nearby, suitable habitat upon daybreak—analogous to a hungry, road-tripping family seeking out the first available rest stop with several restaurants on hand.

Q: *Do migrating birds return to the same backyard feeders each spring and summer?*

A: Many migratory birds display a certain degree of fidelity to their previous nesting or breeding sites. When coupled with their prodigious navigational faculties, it is entirely plausible (and in many cases, likely) that the very birds observed a year ago are again present in the same local backyard or park.

Q: *Why is migration season the best time to see a wide variety of species, and what is migratory fallout?*

A: Many species do not breed or winter locally, with this region instead serving as a waypoint during spring and/or fall migration. This means that many birds are only (or best) observable during certain, migratory months.

Migratory fallout is an event where a large accumulation of birds is observable in a local habitat, often lasting for a few days after a significant weather event. Birds tend to migrate most successfully in the presence of a moderately strong tailwind, with an extended wind of 10-20 mph often serving as the sweet spot. If a favorable wind encourages an above-average number of birds to migrate, and is suddenly interrupted by a major storm, birds will return to ground as soon as possible. With many migrants most active by night, this may lead to a host of activity the following morning—with birds seemingly dripping from every tree branch in sight.

Q: *How do birds survive harsh, northern winters?*

A: Northern-wintering birds have adapted in a variety of ways to survive cold temperatures. Many individuals puff out their feathers and maintain larger fat reserves in an effort to retain more heat, reduce blood flow to the legs to keep their core temperature stable, engage in flocking behavior by day in an effort to locate resources, and some may even roost communally to survive the most frigid of nights.

Q: *Do birds chew their food?*

A: Birds lack teeth, and therefore do not chew in the most conventional sense. Some seed-cracking birds, such as finches, are able to break apart seeds and nuts and eat them in pieces, while raptors are known for tearing apart a fresh kill with their sharp bills. However, large pieces of food are still swallowed, and must be adequately digested.

The solution for birds is a two-stage stomach: with the *gizzard* serving as a second stomach, behind a conventional stomach somewhat resembling that found in many mammals. In species which consume coarser plant materials (e.g., acorns) or hard-shelled invertebrates (e.g., mussels), the gizzard is thick-walled and holds grit and pebbles (which the bird regularly consumes as part of its diet), with the gizzard crushing the mixture to break down otherwise indigestible materials. If present, any harder materials—such as bone, fur, shells, insect exoskeletons, and seed pits—are coalesced into a collected mass, which is coughed up as a *pellet* at a later time. This latter mechanism is most commonly used by larger birds, such as raptors and gulls.

Q: *How do birds bathe?*

A: Birds like to stay clean, too. In areas with sufficient rainfall, individuals commonly bathe by splashing and briefly dunking their heads in puddles and the shallows of ponds, while species in drier climates may give themselves dust baths. These behaviors likely help with feather maintenance. In addition, birds are known to frequently preen themselves throughout the day, with the bill being used to smooth out the feathers and remove small insects.

CONSERVATION

Q: *What is the state of bird conservation efforts today, and are populations decreasing?*

A: Bird conservation efforts may be as organized today as they ever have been, but many global bird populations are still facing an existential threat to their long-term survival. A widely cited, recent study in *Science* found that a staggering three billion birds have been lost from the North American continent over the past 50 years—an overall decline of about 30%. Major threats to avian populations include outdoor housecats (which collectively kill nearly three billion birds in the U.S. and Canada each *year*), habitat loss and redevelopment, pollution, and the use of pesticides and herbicides.

Q: *Have any North American bird species ever been declared extinct?*

A: Unfortunately, yes. In addition to a number of notable subspecies, there are seven species which have been declared extinct in North America over the past 200 years. These include the following, ordered from least to most recent:

- *Great Auk,* a species of coastal water-bird native to the North Atlantic, which likely reached depths of over 250 ft. while diving and measured over 30 in. Some early reports described this bird as the "Northern Penguin," though it was not technically related to the penguins of the Southern Hemisphere. Last confirmed near Iceland, in 1844.

- *Labrador Duck,* a diving duck of the coastal North Atlantic from northeastern Canada to Maryland, which measured about 20 in. Likely uncommon before European colonization. Last confirmed in New York, in 1878.

- *Passenger Pigeon*, a flocking dove of the eastern U.S., which measured about 16 in. Perhaps the most numerous bird in recorded history, with individual flocks reliably estimated at over two billion individuals apiece, and dense nesting colonies covering up to 100 sq. miles. Last confirmed in Indiana, in 1902.

- *Carolina Parakeet*, the only resident North American species of parrot, which ranged throughout the eastern U.S. as far north as New York, and measured about 13 in. This species was hunted as an agricultural pest, a practice which was highly successful due to the parakeets' tendency to return to the fallen members of their flock—perhaps an instinct honed in an effort to collectively swarm predators. Last confirmed in 1904 in Florida, but additional sightings probable through the late 1930s.

- *Ivory-Billed Woodpecker*, a woodpecker larger than the Pileated, which was native to mature, often flooded forests of the Deep South and Cuba and measured about 20 in. This species has been the subject of intensive searches in recent decades, with several unconfirmed reports from the mature, forested swamplands of Louisiana, Arkansas, and Florida. Last confirmed in Louisiana in 1944, and in montane Cuba in 1987.

- *Eskimo Curlew*, a shorebird of the northern tundra which migrated through the Great Plains, measuring about 12 in. May have been among the most numerous North American shorebirds at one point, but was hunted indiscriminately for meat in the late 1800s. Some unconfirmed reports in the last several decades, but last confirmed in Texas in 1962, or in Nebraska in 1987.

- *Bachman's Warbler*, a yellow and gray warbler which bred in flooded forests of the southeastern U.S., and measured about 4 ¼ in. A habitually early migrant, most individuals are thought to have wintered in Cuba. Last confirmed in Louisiana, in 1988.

Q: How have changing habitats due to human development affected birds?

A: With many birds specially adapted for specific ecological niches, the influence of human development has resulted in a set of wide-ranging effects. A few key examples of this are as follows.

Brown-headed Cowbirds, formerly limited to the Great Plains, have been able to move into much of the eastern United States; the fragmentation of wooded habitats for new suburban developments has created vast swaths of fringe habitat perfectly suited for the cowbirds. This species widely practices brood parasitism during the breeding season, wherein the female lays her eggs in a variety of other songbirds' nests, who in turn rear the foreign young. While a natural fixture of its former haunts, this parasitic trait has threatened many species of forest-dwelling sparrows and warblers in its newly acquired ranges.

On the other hand, while much of New England was used for agriculture in the early years of colonization, large tracts of land began to gradually rewild circa 1900 as urban centers began to consolidate around heavy industry. This led to the loss of many grassland and open-habitat species from these areas, such as the Barn Owl and the Bobolink (as well as diminishing populations of the Brown-headed Cowbird), which returned to their former, more westerly ranges—a shift which perfectly illustrates many species' opportunism in embracing new geographies, so long as they match certain habitat criteria.

The practice of replanting forests after they have been logged is laden with additional complications. Many of these replanted forests consist of very few tree species, all of which are fast-growing and planted in such a way to reduce the likelihood of forest fires. However, birds and other animals require a natural diversity of woodland flora, and many other species specialize in transitional woodland (i.e., rewilding habitat full of thickets and saplings). Fires and seemingly unsightly thickets are, in fact, quite normal—therefore, letting nature take its original course is usually the best practice.

It must also be noted that grassland birds, which predominantly inhabit the Great Plains and Midwest, have suffered far greater declines in the past 100 years than many other types of species. This is largely due to the mass cultivation of arable land for agriculture. Unfettered grasslands have been lost at a historic pace, though this has not been discussed as widely: perhaps due to the subtler visual changes to the landscape.

Q: *What are the effects of global warming on the avian world, and what should be expected in the coming decades?*

A: On average, bird populations have been inching northward in past years, with many species moving approximately 10 to 15 miles north per decade. The multifactorial changes to habitat associated with global warming (e.g., melting permafrost, increased forest fires, drying river beds) are likely to only worsen the issue of declining bird populations in future years.

Q: *What are the effects of pesticides?*

A: Pesticides have been one of the primary causes of the precipitous insect declines of the past several decades. Estimates are wide-ranging, but it presently seems that insect populations have decreased by about 40% in the past 50 years. A startling example of this trend is found in the decline of the once-abundant Monarch Butterfly, with populations of this species having declined by well over three-quarters in the past several decades. Collectively, these events have critical trickle-down effects throughout the ecosystem, and are likely a driving factor behind other animal diversity crises.

Q: *How do large glass surfaces and nighttime lighting affect migrating birds?*

A: Lights tend to attract birds, particularly during nocturnal migration flights. This, in combination with the large glass windows which tend to accompany nighttime lighting in urban areas, has led to masses of stunned and deceased birds falling to the pavement in cities all throughout North America. As many as one billion birds die each year in the U.S. due to window strikes of this nature. To combat this issue, many cities have recently launched campaigns to introduce bird-friendly windows and auto-off lighting in tall office buildings.

IDENTIFICATION

Q: *I saw a fully or partially white bird at my feeders. What are leucism, albinism, and melanism?*

A: Both leucism and albinism can result in the manifestation of unusual whiteness. Leucism results in partial pigmentation, with some feathers developing normally and others becoming a patchy white. This is far more common than albinism, which is a rare condition in which all feathers are white and the eyes are a washed-out pink; this is due to a complete inability to produce pigmentation.

Leucistic female Boat-tailed Grackle pictured above.
Note that a normal individual would be fully brown and black.

Melanism, on the other hand, involves overactive pigment production, wherein the bird has a visibly darker (or even blackish) appearance. This condition is likely rarer than both leucism and albinism.

White-winged Dove exhibiting melanism above. Note that this species is normally a pale taupe (i.e., similar to Mourning Dove), rather than brown as pictured.

In addition, the exceptionally rare case of xanthochroism, or xanthism, results in excessively yellow individuals. This is normally due to a genetic condition, but could theoretically be rooted in dietary causes as well.

Q: *How often do birds molt their feathers?*

A: Most birds molt their flight feathers—or *remiges*—once each year, and molt their body feathers one or two times per year.

Q: *What are breeding and nonbreeding plumages, and for which months does each term apply?*

A: Breeding plumage is often displayed by adults from April until August; this plumage demonstrates the health or virility of potential mates, and may be incorporated into some courtship rituals. Nonbreeding plumage, on the other hand, is usually displayed from August through March. The nonbreeding plumage is normally duller, so as to reduce visibility from potential predators throughout the remainder of the year.

BACKYARDS AND BIRD FEEDERS

Q: *What should I do with an injured bird?*

A: If an injured bird is located, particularly in the backyard, it is normally best to leave it alone for a short period. However, if the individual is alive but remains immobilized, a conscientious birder should locate and contact a local wildlife rehabilitation clinic for further instructions.

Q: *How have bird feeders contributed to the size and distribution of bird populations?*

A: Casually scattering seeds on the ground for birds has been practiced since the first millennium, A.D., but dedicated bird feeders only came on the scene in the early 1900s, with widespread adoption picking up in the middle decades of the 20th Century. Some species which were previously observed at more southerly latitudes, such as the Northern Cardinal and Tufted Titmouse, are common today throughout the Great Lakes and Northeast, while Mourning Doves now stay the winter across both of these regions. Many other populations of native, feeder-visiting species have been bolstered by this rising tide as well. However, feeders are widely blamed for accelerating the spread of the House Finch throughout the eastern U.S., in addition to abetting the localized explosions of invasive House Sparrow populations.

In short, feeders have dramatically impacted the avian landscape, but in more good ways than bad.

Q: *Which birds are more likely to push around others at a contested feeder?*

A: In general, larger birds tend to best assert their dominance when visiting crowded feeders. However, woodpeckers tend to frequently displace larger birds, and House Finches often outcompete slightly larger Purple Finches.

Note: For additional information on this subtopic, please see the previous section, entitled "Introduction to Birding and Bird Feeding."

THE
BIRDS

③ **GREAT BLUE HERON.** *Ardea herodias.*

SIZE: 45 in.

HABITAT: Coastlines, wetlands, rivers, sometimes fields.

WILD DIET: Primarily fish, though various aquatic wildlife—as well as small mammals and ducklings—may sometimes be taken.

BEHAVIOR: Often observed standing motionless at the edge of bodies of water, waiting for prey. When a nearby fish is spotted, the heron normally strikes from a standing position; however, individuals sometimes chase after their quarry by briskly walking through the water, with head cocked. These birds are usually only seen by suburbanites as they fly from one feeding location to another, though they are among the most common and easily observable wetland birds of this region. Flying motion is languid and wingbeats are somewhat labored, with long legs extended behind.

MIGRATE? Mostly.

NESTING: Typically nests in groups (known as heronries) in remote areas, particularly in and atop trees, though some may build nests in safe locations at ground level. Sticks and vegetative debris are used to build a bulky platform. About 2-4 ft. across, and up to 2 ft. thick.

EGGS: Light blue. Length of 2 ½ - 3 in. Total of 3-5.

FEEDER BEHAVIOR: Does not visit feeders.

COMPARE TO SIMILAR SPECIES: Large size and dull blue-to-gray coloration distinguishes this species from other large wading birds. Trailing legs, as well as slow and direct flying motion, differentiate from Turkey Vulture in flight.

DID YOU KNOW? While the Great Blue Heron primarily hunts in the calm shallows, some regional populations have developed their own unique approaches. For instance, individuals on the west coast of North America have been known to stand atop floating kelp beds while hunting, and some in the southeastern U.S. have even adapted to hunt in intertidal zones amid high, rolling waves.

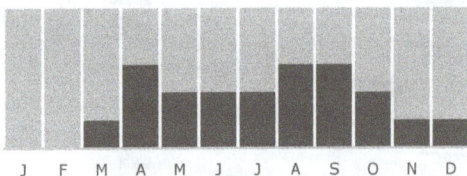

J F M A M J J A S O N D

Adults at top and bottom.

Male displaying at top (Photo by Vince Pahkala / CC BY-SA / Cropped),
Female with juveniles at bottom (Photo by D. Gordon E. Robertson / CC BY-SA / Cropped).

② **WILD TURKEY.** *Meleagris gallopavo*.

SIZE: 39 in.

HABITAT: Edges of woods, especially near clearings and fields.

WILD DIET: Nuts, large seeds, berries, insects and spiders, and occasionally small reptiles and amphibians.

BEHAVIOR: Active foragers, typically walking along the ground. To locate the nuts and seeds which it usually takes for food, individuals often scratch away leaf litter from the forest floor in an effort to uncover any unclaimed morsels. These tidbits are stored along with an assortment of gravelly rocks in the turkey's large gizzard, which slowly grinds the plant matter into more readily digestible pieces. In winter, this portly bird— with males weighing in excess of 15 pounds—may even climb into evergreens to search for any unclaimed food sources.

MIGRATE? No.

NESTING: Areas surrounded by thick shrubbery or tree growth are typically chosen, though some individuals have been known to nest in overgrown fields. An inch-deep depression in the soil is scraped away, upon which the female lays and incubates her eggs. About 12-18 in. across.

EGGS: Light yellow or tan, with red and brown flecks. Length of 2 - 2 ½ in. Total of 8-16.

FEEDER BEHAVIOR: Does not visit feeders, but may be attracted to backyards with native nut-bearing or berry vegetation, particularly if there is nearby woodland.

COMPARE TO SIMILAR SPECIES: Distinctive, and unlike many other birds of this region.

DID YOU KNOW? Wild Turkeys lack adequate night vision, and therefore must roost in trees at night to avoid predators. Individuals have been observed as high as 50 feet above the ground, often selecting some of the highest available perches available in a sturdy, older-growth tree.

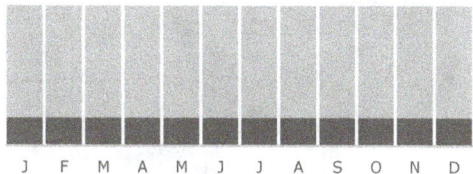

J F M A M J J A S O N D

① **GREAT EGRET.** *Ardea alba*.

SIZE: 38 in.

HABITAT: Usually wetlands, but also calm rivers, lakes, ponds, and sections of coastline—particularly where wetland-like conditions persist.

WILD DIET: Mostly small fish and frogs, but also small mammals, insects, birds, and reptiles.

BEHAVIOR: Often observed standing motionless in the shallows of a pond or marsh, waiting to strike a fish that swims its way. This species' feeding technique is similar to that of the Great Blue Heron, with individuals either standing still in wait, or slowly wading into the fringes of schooling fish; this preambulatory stalking culminates with a sudden strike of the bill into the water, after which the fish is swallowed whole in a series of occasionally cumbersome, stepwise motions. Flies with long, lumbering wingbeats as it moves between feeding locations: one must watch for its cocked neck and long, trailing legs. A rattling, croaking call may also be given during these brief aerial excursions.

MIGRATE? Yes.

NESTING: Nests colonially in trees overlooking wetlands, situated dozens of feet off the ground. Platform is constructed of sticks and lined with grasses. About 2-3 ft. across and 8 in. deep.

EGGS: Pale blue or green. Length of 2 ½ in. Total of 3-5.

FEEDER BEHAVIOR: Does not visit feeders.

COMPARE TO SIMILAR SPECIES: Most similar to Snowy Egrets or juvenile Little Blue Herons, but the larger size of the Great Egret is the best and most obvious differentiator.

DID YOU KNOW? While this species does not naturally occur in Europe, it has been known to occasionally wander east of its normal range. In the past decade alone, breeding pairs of Great Egrets have successfully reproduced and potentially begun to establish themselves in the British Isles and in Scandinavia.

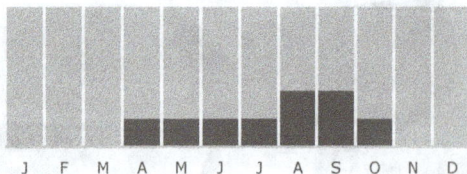

J F M A M J J A S O N D

Adults at top and bottom.

Adult at top,
Adult with juveniles, or goslings, at bottom.

④ **CANADA GOOSE.** *Branta canadensis*.

SIZE: 37 in.
HABITAT: Shallows of ponds and lakes, wetlands, and large fields.
WILD DIET: Various grasses and grains, occasionally insects and small fish.
BEHAVIOR: Often seen in large flocks, particularly flying overhead in V-formation while insouciantly honking. The V-formation is typically employed to decrease wind resistance while affording each individual a forward view; throughout longer flights, the geese will cycle positions to more equally share the workload. Prefers to graze in large fields and lawns, or while floating in aquatic habitat, often near the shallows. This species has adapted very well to human development, with many individuals no longer migrating to the southern U.S. for the winter, as had always been the case before. Consequently, Canada Geese are now commonly observed in the lawns abutting office parks, near urban ponds, or in a variety of other well-populated areas. However, individuals may be aggressive toward humans if they feel threatened, and it is therefore best to always keep a safe distance.
MIGRATE? Partially.
NESTING: A slightly elevated area is chosen, upon which a shallow, bowl-shaped nest is constructed of loose vegetation and lined with feathers. About 1 ½ - 2 ft. across.
EGGS: Off-white. Length of 3 in. Total of 3-7.
FEEDER BEHAVIOR: Does not visit feeders.

COMPARE TO SIMILAR SPECIES: The far less common Cackling Goose has similar markings, though this species has a much shorter neck, stubbier bill, and is closer to 25 in. in length on average.

DID YOU KNOW? Canada Geese are among the most common birds to be struck by aircraft, likely due to their flocking behavior and tendency to feed in large fields. It has been estimated that these birds have caused tens of millions of dollars' worth of damage to aircraft in the United States in the past few decades, though predator decoys and habitat relocation efforts have been moderately effective in recent years.

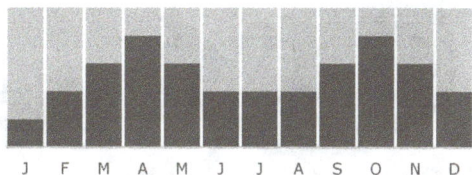

J F M A M J J A S O N D

① **BALD EAGLE.** *Haliaeetus leucocephalus.*

SIZE: 34 in.

HABITAT: Coastlines of various bodies of water (e.g., rivers, lakes, reservoirs, and oceans), particularly with adjacent, mature woods.

WILD DIET: Mostly fish (usually up to 24 in. in size), but also carrion, other birds, and mammals.

BEHAVIOR: Flies with powerful, regal wingbeats, and often selects high or open perches in tall, mature trees. Frequently captures fish by swooping low and extending its talons just beneath the water's surface, though some eagles may also harass other predators (e.g., ospreys, gulls, and even otters) to steal a fresh catch. The spectacular courtship displays of this bird are among the most widely discussed in the avian world, with male and female locking talons in midair before tumbling downward together—only separating at the final moment to avoid striking the ground.

MIGRATE? Partially.

NESTING: Often selects mature conifers, with optimal location near the top. Sticks and grasses are used to construct a nest, or eyrie, that may grow to be as large as 8 ft. wide and deep, and over a ton in weight. Breeding pairs typically return to the same nests each year.

EGGS: Various shades of white. Length of 3 in. Total of 2-3.

FEEDER BEHAVIOR: Does not visit feeders.

COMPARE TO SIMILAR SPECIES: Juveniles may be confused with large hawks or Golden Eagles. To distinguish, note the mottled, dirty coloration of feathers and the fingered ends of wings. However, the white markings of adults are very much distinct.

DID YOU KNOW? Though Bald Eagles numbered well into the hundreds of thousands as recently as the mid-1800s, hunting and DDT pesticide use reduced the total number of nesting pairs in the contiguous U.S. to under 500 by the 1950s. Federal protections have since allowed these populations to recover, with over 300,000 individuals present in the Lower 48 today: a figure that is expected to continue to increase, as long as adequate protections remain. Furthermore, Bald Eagles are now so numerous in the Aleutian Islands that locals of Dutch Harbor, Alaska have taken to calling them "Dutch Harbor pigeons."

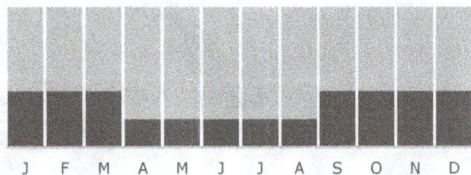

J F M A M J J A S O N D

Adult at top,
Juvenile at bottom (Photo by KetaDesign / CC BY-SA).

Adult swimming at top,
Adult resting at bottom left (Photo by Frank Schulenberg / CC BY-SA / Cropped),
Juvenile at bottom right (Photo by Virginia State Parks / CC BY-SA / Cropped).

② DOUBLE-CRESTED CORMORANT.
Phalacrocorax auritus.

SIZE: 32 in.

HABITAT: Coastlines, harbors, large lakes and rivers. Infrequently found in smaller lakes, ponds, and wetlands.

WILD DIET: Mostly fish (up to 12 in. in size).

BEHAVIOR: Often observed sitting low in the water before swiftly diving to hunt for prey. This species may swim as deep as 50 feet in search of food. Individuals also form large, conspicuous flocks on piers and sandbars as they dry their feathers in the sun. These flocks collectively consume a great quantity of fish, with each cormorant ingurgitating about one pound of food daily; consequently, cormorant populations in the Great Lakes alone take nearly 80 million pounds of fish yearly.

MIGRATE? Yes.

NESTING: Colonial nesters, usually selecting locations in trees or on protected rocky shorelines. Bowl-shaped, and comprised of twigs and feathers. About 2 ft. in diameter and 8 in. high.

EGGS: Off-white, possibly with shades of pale blue. Length of 2 ½ in. Total of 1-6.

FEEDER BEHAVIOR: Does not visit feeders.

COMPARE TO SIMILAR SPECIES: The adult Great Cormorant is slightly larger and stockier through the body, and has a white flank patch and white patch behind the bill; meanwhile, juvenile Greats have mostly white bellies, and juvenile Double-cresteds only have white on the upper chest. The Neotropic Cormorant is much smaller and also has a proportionately smaller head and bill.

DID YOU KNOW? Double-crested Cormorants are not particularly gracious tenants. After several years of reusing nests in a given tree, the excessive guano buildup on the ground beneath will often kill the tree outright, forcing the nesters to move to another nearby site.

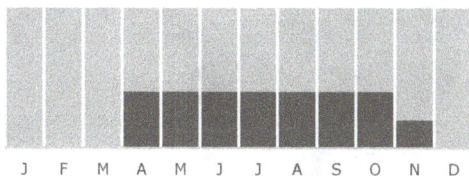

J F M A M J J A S O N D

① COMMON LOON (or GREAT NORTHERN DIVER). *Gavia immer.*

SIZE: 31 in.

HABITAT: Mostly deep, medium- to large-sized lakes, and oceanic coastlines.

WILD DIET: Fish (e.g., bass, sunfish, and walleye).

BEHAVIOR: As with the grebes, this species has legs which are set far behind the body's center of gravity, making for awkward land-based walking but prolific swimming abilities. Individuals have been known to make split-second changes of direction, rapid propulsive movements, and quick gyrations around underwater obstacles in pursuit of prey, which are brought to the surface and engulfed headfirst. Their high degree of wing-loading requires long takeoff areas for flight, thus necessitating larger bodies of water for feeding.

MIGRATE? Partially.

NESTING: Chooses a quiet, sheltered site on the shore, usually on a small island. A mound with an inner bowl is formed from wet vegetative debris, and may reach sizes of up to 2 ft. across.

EGGS: Yellow-brown with dirty blotches. Length of 3 ½ in. Total of 2.

FEEDER BEHAVIOR: Does not visit feeders, but may use nesting platforms.

COMPARE TO SIMILAR SPECIES: Larger than other North American loons, breeding adults have distinct head plumage with a jet-black bill. Nonbreeding adults are well identified from the side, with the demarcation between dark and white coloration along the neck somewhat patchy and irregular (the Pacific Loon has a nearly straight line), though roughly along the median.

DID YOU KNOW? This species is perhaps most famous for its whooping, whistling yodels and wails, which have ethereally drifted over the surfaces of placid lakeshores and coastlines for millennia. It has also featured in many traditions of Native American spiritual folklore, and on the Canadian one-dollar coin.

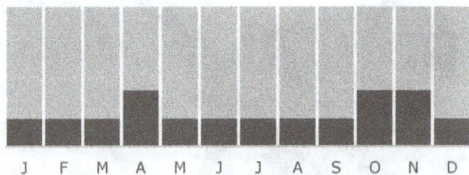

J F M A M J J A S O N D

Breeding adults swimming at top,
Nonbreeding adult at bottom.

Snow/white adult at top,
Blue adult at bottom (Photo by Trish Hartmann / CC BY-SA / Cropped).

① SNOW GOOSE. *Anser caerulescens*.

SIZE: 30 in.

HABITAT: Shallows of lakes and ponds, wetlands, and fields. In summer, breeds in the far northern tundra.

WILD DIET: Various aquatic vegetation and agricultural grains. Sometimes, fruits and berries.

BEHAVIOR: Often found loitering or noisily honking in very large flocks, this species forages in the shallows of wetlands or bays, or gleans waste grains from agricultural fields. Though flocks tend to fly at very high altitudes, they may sometimes be observed swirling and settling into a communal roosting location—a truly spectacular sight. At night, individuals may roost floating on the water, sitting, or standing one-legged. Common predators across much of their range include mammals ranging in size from foxes to bears, as well as eagles.

MIGRATE? Yes.

NESTING: Colonial nester. Selects a high-ground location, often near a pond or bog. A shallow nest scrape is lined with grasses and feathers. Up to 3 ft. across.

EGGS: Shades of white, with older eggs more heavily stained. Length of 3 in. Total of 3-6.

FEEDER BEHAVIOR: Does not visit feeders.

COMPARE TO SIMILAR SPECIES: The uncommon, smaller Ross's Goose is very similar, with notable differences including the following: the Ross's has a blunter bill with bluish coloring behind the nostrils; lacks a blackish, grin-like opening between the upper and lower bill; and *lacks a distinct curve along the vertical base of the bill.*

DID YOU KNOW? There are actually two color morphs of the Snow Goose: the white Snow, and the much less common Blue. The Blue morph features mostly dark plumage from the lower neck down.

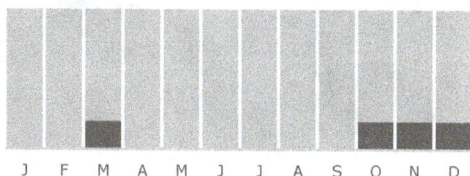

J F M A M J J A S O N D

④ TURKEY VULTURE. *Cathartes aura*.

SIZE: 28 in.

HABITAT: Sparse woods, open fields, roadsides, landfills.

WILD DIET: Carrion, human garbage (up to one-quarter of total dietary intake may consist of artificial materials inadvertently consumed at landfills).

BEHAVIOR: Slowly, wobblingly flies and circles above the countryside, with its long, broad wings held in a shallow V-shape. Throughout the day, this species takes advantage of rising currents of warm air, which enable individuals to effortlessly glide along with very few, if any, wingbeats; these currents, known as *thermals*, are also used by other raptors, such as Red-tailed Hawks, as they scan the countryside for food. Once several 50-degree days occur in a row, Turkey Vultures tend to migrate south for the winter, given that the strength of thermal currents proportionately decreases with daytime temperatures. Solitary individuals or small groups may be observed feeding on carrion along abandoned roadsides.

MIGRATE? Yes.

NESTING: Little to no nest construction. Selects rocky openings, such as caves and crevices, as well as hollowed trees and animal burrows.

EGGS: Milky white with irregular red-brown spotting. Length of 3 in. Total of 2.

FEEDER BEHAVIOR: Does not visit feeders, though can be attracted by animal carcasses.

COMPARE TO SIMILAR SPECIES: The Black Vulture lacks the black-and-tan pattern on the underwing, as well as a red head.

DID YOU KNOW? Turkey Vultures are one of the few birds to possess a sense of smell, by which it finds its food sources. Interestingly, natural gas maintenance employees have repeatedly reported Turkey Vultures congregating en masse after pipelines have burst. This is due to the presence of the natural gas additive ethyl mercaptan, which is also released by decaying flesh.

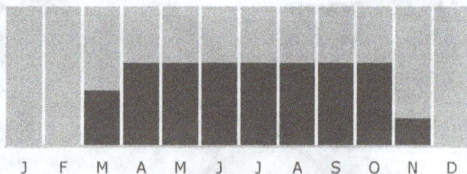

J F M A M J J A S O N D

Adult perching at top (Photo by Devra Cooper / CC BY-SA),
Soaring at bottom.

Adult loafing at top,
Adult hunting at bottom (fish pictured is a flounder).

① GREAT BLACK-BACKED GULL. *Larus marinus.*

SIZE: 28 in.

HABITAT: Coastlines, often of large bodies of water (e.g., Lake Champlain). Also, landfills.

WILD DIET: Mostly fish, but also garbage at landfills, other birds, and aquatic invertebrates.

BEHAVIOR: Active forager at the surface of water and at garbage dumps. Historically limited to the oceanic coastlines of the North Atlantic, droves of Great Black-backed Gulls have been moving inland to the Great Lakes, supported by the usage of garbage dumps as supplementary—or even primary—feeding sites. Often observed milling around large parking lots and piers, particularly in mixed flocks of gulls.

MIGRATE? Partially, with some individuals remaining year-round.

NESTING: Prefers to select islands or other locations less accessible to predators. Vegetation and garbage are often used as nest materials, which are placed atop a raised object, such as a large rock or a tree stump.

EGGS: Tan, brown, or brown-green, with dark speckles. Length of 3 in. Total of 2-3.

FEEDER BEHAVIOR: Does not visit feeders.

COMPARE TO SIMILAR SPECIES: This is the largest of all gull species, and is identifiable by the dark gray-to-black coloration on the upper side of wings. Individuals are best differentiated from the less common Lesser Black-Backed Gull by notable size difference and leg color (the Lesser features bright yellow, rather than dull pink, legs).

DID YOU KNOW? A voracious predator of seemingly anything that will fit in its mouth, the Great Black-Backed Gull is one of the only gull species which actively hunts smaller birds. This behavior is most common throughout the breeding season, when abundant nestlings and fledglings often prove to be an easy meal. However, adults sometimes also pursue seabirds such as puffins, as well as terrestrial songbirds up to 12 inches in length.

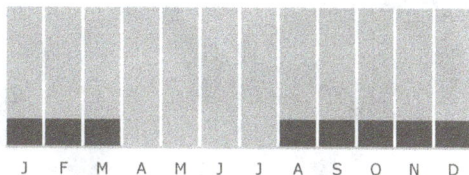

J F M A M J J A S O N D

② COMMON MERGANSER. *Mergus merganser.*

SIZE: 25 in.

HABITAT: Lakes, rivers, streams, and ponds, especially if near mature, dense woods.

WILD DIET: Mostly fish, but also aquatic invertebrates, amphibians, and occasionally small mammals or birds.

BEHAVIOR: This species is a diving duck, which means that it fully submerges and swims underwater when in search of prey. It may stay underwater for up to a minute, and grasps its prey with the serrated edges of its bill. Known for organized group hunting as well, whereby the mergansers chase a fish into shallow water for easier capture. Spends most of its time on the water.

MIGRATE? Partially.

NESTING: Cavity nesters, usually selecting a nest near wetlands with an entrance hole at least 6 in. in diameter. May place loose vegetation, feathers on the floor.

EGGS: White or whitish-tan. Length of 2 ½ in. Total of 8-13.

FEEDER BEHAVIOR: Does not visit feeders, but does use nest boxes.

COMPARE TO SIMILAR SPECIES: Red-breasted Merganser also features males with green heads and females with red heads, with similar silhouette. However, male Common Mergansers have a white body (apart from upper back) and lack a reddish breast; meanwhile, male Red-breasteds have brown and white sides, a trailing tuft on the head, and a white stripe on neck with red-brown upper chest. In addition, female Commons have darker head and neck coloration than their Red-breasted counterparts.

DID YOU KNOW? Gulls—and even some raptors—are known to shadow flocks of Common Mergansers in hopes of stealing any captured prey once the ducks surface. This practice is known as *kleptoparasitism.*

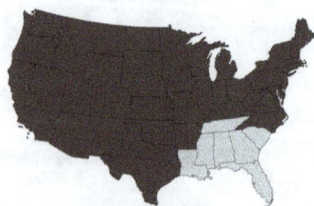

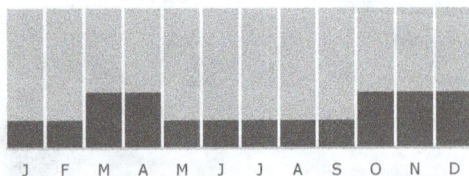

J F M A M J J A S O N D

Male at top,
Female at bottom.

Male at top,
Two males with female at bottom.

① NORTHERN PINTAIL. *Anas acuta.*

SIZE: 25 in.

HABITAT: Shallows of open wetlands, flooded fields and marshes, lakes.

WILD DIET: Seeds and roots of aquatic plants, aquatic invertebrates, and terrestrial grains and seeds.

BEHAVIOR: This species is a member of the dabbling ducks, and thus periodically tips forward to feed, submerging its head and neck underwater. It mostly feeds at dusk or nighttime. The Northern Pintail's long neck, especially compared to those of some other dabbling ducks, allows it to reach more than one foot beneath the surface for vegetation. However, pintails are frequently observed in the muddy shallows of ephemeral ponds and puddles, rooting in the substrate for vegetation. Like other waterfowl, this species molts its feathers in late summer and temporarily becomes flightless; in response, most Northern Pintails remain secretive for this period. Individuals may be spotted walking about in agricultural fields or meadows during the winter, searching for grains and seeds.

MIGRATE? Yes.

NESTING: Ground nester, sometimes far from water. Scrapes an impression into the ground, upon which loose, matted grasses are placed. About 9 in. wide and 3 in. deep.

EGGS: Shades of white, possibly with dirty mottling. Length of 2 in. Total of 6-9.

FEEDER BEHAVIOR: Does not visit feeders.

COMPARE TO SIMILAR SPECIES: Male's long tail and distinct head and neck markings allow for a simple identification. Female is often situated near males, but the dark gray bill and brown-and-white feathered sides should be noticed.

DID YOU KNOW? Long-distance migrants, this species can fly for up to 2,000 miles nonstop and at speeds of up to 50 mph: perhaps even faster in the presence of a forceful tailwind. Its breeding grounds range from the Arctic Circle to the northern U.S., and its wintering grounds are as far south as Central America and the Caribbean.

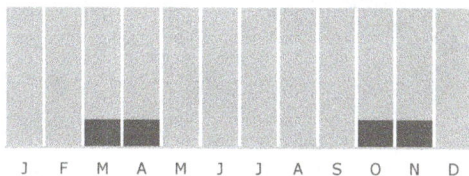

J F M A M J J A S O N D

② HERRING GULL. *Larus argentatus.*

SIZE: 24 in.

HABITAT: Coastlines, wetlands, landfills, picnic areas.

WILD DIET: Aquatic invertebrates, fish, worms, carrion, garbage at landfills.

BEHAVIOR: Opportunistic, undiscerning forager at the surface of water, in mudflats and tidal areas, at garbage dumps, and sometimes near urban habitation. Often seen milling around large parking lots, piers, and plowed fields, particularly in mixed flocks of gulls. This gull, like the Ring-billed Gull in particular, has adapted remarkably well to human development. Some individuals have been noted to observe humans for extended periods, with possible benefits including the learning and memorization of various urban threats, as well as the mimicking of human food preferences.

MIGRATE? Partially.

NESTING: A cluster of small craters is scraped away in the dirt or sand, one for each individual egg, and lined with vegetation, garbage, and/or feathers. Often hidden behind an obstruction, such as a bush or large rock.

EGGS: Light green-blue to brown with dark speckles. Length of 3 in. Total of 2-3.

FEEDER BEHAVIOR: Does not visit feeders.

COMPARE TO SIMILAR SPECIES: Most similar to Ring-billed Gull. Note the Herring's pale, pink legs, contrasting with the bright yellow legs of the Ring-billed. Also, the Herring is more stockily built, larger, and adults possess a large, red dot on the lower bill.

DID YOU KNOW? As is the case with most gulls, as well as many other seabirds, the Herring Gull can drink salty seawater without complaint. It possesses specialized salt glands near its eyes, which drain directly through the nostrils and allow for the filtered excess salt to be safely secreted. Remarkably, a single gull has the ability to safely filter up to one-quarter of a pound of saline seawater every two hours.

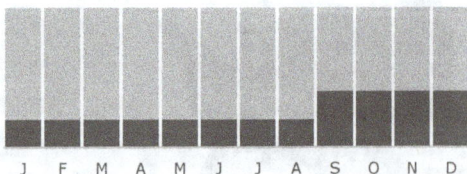

J F M A M J J A S O N D

Adult in breeding plumage at top (Photo by Dick Daniels / CC BY-SA)
(Note: Nonbreeding plumage features dirty gray streaking along the head and neck),
Subadult at bottom.

Perching adult at top (Photo by David Hofmann / CC BY-SA),
Flying adult at bottom (Photo by Tom Koerner / CC BY-SA / Cropped).

③ **COMMON RAVEN.** *Corvus corax.*

SIZE: 24 in.

HABITAT: Nearly anywhere, but often prefers various undisturbed woods.

WILD DIET: Nearly anything, including small animals and birds, carrion, grains and seeds, insects and spiders, garbage, and occasionally mammal dung.

BEHAVIOR: Among the most intelligent birds, and perhaps animals, on Earth. Engages in sophisticated communication, problem-solving, deception, and luring techniques, among other behaviors. Often in groups of two, though individuals may cooperatively flock in the winter: particularly in areas with larger raven populations. This species typically forms diet specializations based on what is most commonly available in its territory; for instance, ravens present in open country tend to most often feed on roadkill, ravens found near suburbs appear to specialize in the removal of food waste from garbage dumps and dumpsters, and forest-dwelling ravens are most adept at locating, seizing, and caching insects, nuts, and seeds. Additionally, lone individuals or pairs may be the victims of territorial mobbing behaviors exhibited by hordes of American Crows, which often provide a telling clue as to the raven's nearby presence.

MIGRATE? No.

NESTING: Sticks are woven together to form a nest up to 4 ft. in diameter, and up to 2 ft. deep. Mud and vegetation are used inside of the nest. Nests may be reused, but not necessarily by the same pairs.

EGGS: Light blue-green with brown splotching. Length of 2 in. Total of 3-7.

FEEDER BEHAVIOR: May occasionally scavenge beneath feeders.

COMPARE TO SIMILAR SPECIES: Most similar to American Crow, but much larger. In addition, the Common Raven has a thicker bill, a distinct wedge-shaped tail (nearly triangular at the end) when unfurled, fluffier head and neck feathers, a more graceful flight pattern, and a guttural croaking call.

DID YOU KNOW? Some ravens have been known to loudly mimic the vocalizations of canids upon finding a fresh carcass. After the predators have been lured to the site, torn apart the flesh, and departed, the waiting ravens eagerly scavenge the remains.

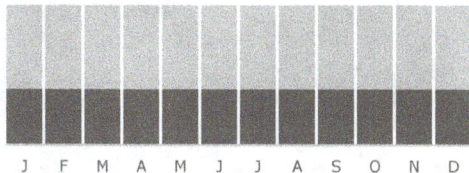

J F M A M J J A S O N D

③ **MALLARD.** *Anas platyrhynchos.*

SIZE: 23 in.

HABITAT: Wetlands, shallows of lakes and ponds, parks, and fields.

WILD DIET: Seeds, grains, and human-offered food (though offering food is not recommended). Also, aquatic and terrestrial insects, invertebrates.

BEHAVIOR: This species is a dabbling duck, feeding by dipping its head and neck underwater. Like other waterfowl, this species does not possess teeth inside its bill; instead, it periodically swallows pebbles and gravel, which accumulate in the gizzard and help to churn plant matter into more digestible tidbits. Mallards are adaptable foragers, and will often visit fields or parks where human activity has left food scraps, particularly bread crumbs—though these are not healthy for the birds. In parks with a high degree of human contact, these birds will often be quite comfortable around people.

MIGRATE? Partially.

NESTING: Ground nester. Scrapes a small depression in the ground, upon which loose vegetation and eggs are laid. About 9 in. wide and 3 in. deep.

EGGS: White to light blue-green. Length of 2-2 ½ in. Total of 6-13.

FEEDER BEHAVIOR: Does not visit feeders.

COMPARE TO SIMILAR SPECIES: Male is distinctive, but female can be confused with females of other dabbling duck species. American Black Duck females are darker in the body than female Mallards, and also have a dull green tint to the bill.

DID YOU KNOW? Mallards are known for readily breeding with ducks of other species, producing hybrid offspring that can prove an unusual challenge to identify. Species that have hybridized with Mallards include Northern Shovelers (e.g., producing Northern Shoveler x Mallard offspring), Wood Ducks, Northern Pintails, Common Eiders, Green-winged Teals, Gadwalls, and many others.

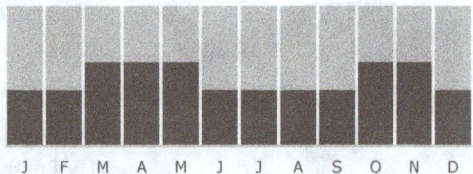

J F M A M J J A S O N D

Male at top,
Female at bottom (Photo by Jamain / CC BY-SA).

Adults with fresh kill at top and bottom.

② OSPREY. *Pandion haliaetus.*

SIZE: 23 in.

HABITAT: Lakes, bays, rivers, and wetlands.

WILD DIET: Fish (less than 18 in. in length).

BEHAVIOR: When hunting, flies as high as 100 feet above areas of shallow water (with wings held in an M-shape), searching for prey below. Once spotted, the individual enters a steep, aerodynamic dive with talons outstretched, piercing the surface of the water upon impact and grasping the fish. This process is repeated with remarkable efficiency; when an osprey is situated in a habitat with sufficient food sources, it frequently seizes a fish in just 10 minutes, and a few dives, of hunting. Often also called seahawks, bayhawks, riverhawks, and fish-hawks, referencing their distinct ecological niche.

MIGRATE? Yes.

NESTING: Selects a high fork of a tree, a clifftop, or a manmade nesting platform. A loose, roughshod platform of sticks. May be reused. About 3-5 ft. wide and up to 3 ft. deep after many years of use and additions.

EGGS: Light yellow-brown with red or brown splotches. Length of 2 ½ in. Total of 1-4.

FEEDER BEHAVIOR: Does not visit feeders.

COMPARE TO SIMILAR SPECIES: Much smaller than the Bald Eagle. If observed in an area with many gulls present, notice the distinct markings of this species; additionally, if carrying prey, the Osprey holds fish in its talons—rather than gulls, which hold prey with their bills.

DID YOU KNOW? The Osprey is one of the only raptor species in the world with a reversible outer toe, which allows for this species to have two toes on both the front and back when gripping slimy, wet fish prey. Ospreys also possess small, barb-like grips on the pads of their feet, which allow for an even more secure hold.

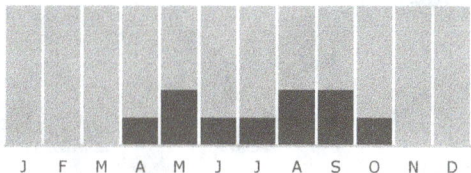

J F M A M J J A S O N D

② AMERICAN BLACK DUCK. *Anas rubripes.*

SIZE: 22 in.

HABITAT: Wetlands.

WILD DIET: Aquatic vegetation and invertebrates.

BEHAVIOR: A dabbling duck, this species will repeatedly upend itself when foraging. This species is somewhat unique, however, in that it will sometimes dive as well—both to avoid predators and to reach vegetation in deeper waters. Individuals often have a strong affinity to their usual wintering sites, occasionally starving rather than leaving a frozen-over wetland that has been visited in past years. Additionally, like other dabbling ducks, the American Black Duck can take flight directly from a floating position, allowing for a quick getaway from any perceived threat; this is unlike the behavior of diving ducks, which frequently must perform a running start while sufficient momentum is generated for flight.

MIGRATE? Partially.

NESTING: Nests on the ground in a well-sheltered location, or very occasionally in tree cavities. A shallow depression is formed, upon which loose vegetation and feathers are placed.

EGGS: White. Length of 2 ½ in. Total of 8-14, occasionally with a second brood.

FEEDER BEHAVIOR: Does not visit feeders.

COMPARE TO SIMILAR SPECIES: Darker than Mallards, with a duller bill color. Darker than Mottled Duck, with a brown head (rather than tan). Gadwall is smaller with a gray body in males, and a moderately brown body in females.

DID YOU KNOW? Though not yet on the roster of endangered species, this duck has experienced declines as steep as 90% over the past half-century. This may largely owe to the fact that its preferred wooded wetland habitats are increasingly scarce due to deforestation and human development.

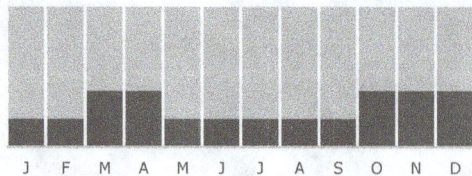

J F M A M J J A S O N D

Male at top (Photo by Dick Daniels / CC BY-SA),
Female at bottom (Photo by Dick Daniels / CC BY-SA).

Perching adult at top,
Soaring adult at bottom (Photo by Tom Koerner / CC BY-SA).

③ **RED-TAILED HAWK.** *Buteo jamaicensis.*

SIZE: 22 in.

HABITAT: Nearly anywhere, but prefers open woods, fields, and roadsides.

WILD DIET: Mostly small mammals (in particular, squirrels). Less frequently, birds, reptiles, and carrion.

BEHAVIOR: Often observed soaring or circling gracefully in the sky, with light wingbeats, though individuals also perch in trees or on telephone poles. While driving along a highway or interstate, this species is commonly present in perches along the roadside—much more visible in winter, after most leaves have fallen. The Red-tailed Hawk, like many raptors, possesses phenomenal visual acuity; a lone squirrel darting through brush and long grass can be spotted from up to 300 feet away. Once its quarry has been sighted, the hawk swoops low with strong wingbeats, culminating with a forceful strike of the talons, which may stun the prey. Upon its secure capture, the hawk normally carries its prey to a safe perch for consumption. Its familiar, piercing call is often heard in the background of Western-genre films, and is usually given in flight.

MIGRATE? Mostly not, though some individuals may vacate northern Vermont in the colder months.

NESTING: Typically situated atop a large tree or similarly habitable human-made structure (e.g., billboards). Piles of sticks up to 3 ft. across, and up to 5 ft. deep.

EGGS: White, with some brown blotching. Length of 2 ½ in. Total of 2-5.

FEEDER BEHAVIOR: Uncommonly hunts near feeders.

COMPARE TO SIMILAR SPECIES: Similar to Red-shouldered Hawk in shape, but note pale undersides, dark band of streaking across upper belly (which may be lighter or splotchier in juveniles, but is still present), and light red coloration on tail.

DID YOU KNOW? The ancient practice of falconry, whereby humans train captive raptors to hunt animals on their behalf, is continued today by nearly 5,000 Americans: who must first secure a regulatory permit and a registered sponsor. The Red-tailed Hawk, along with the Red-shouldered Hawk, is one of only two North American hawks approved for use by trainees or apprentices; consequently, the Red-tailed is also the most common raptor used by North American falconers, with some hawks adapting to trained hunting techniques in a mere two weeks.

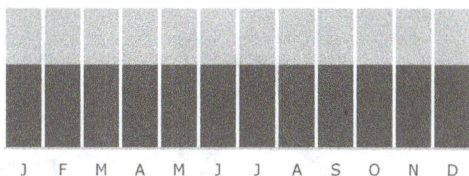

| J | F | M | A | M | J | J | A | S | O | N | D |

59

① **CASPIAN TERN.** *Hydroprogne caspia.*

SIZE: 20 in.

HABITAT: Coastlines of oceans, large lakes, and large rivers.

WILD DIET: Mostly fish, occasionally invertebrates and large insects.

BEHAVIOR: Flies overwater as it scans below for fish beneath the surface. When suitable prey is sighted, the tern will hover with wings outstretched as it prepares to plunge bill-first, reaching a depth of up to two feet before quickly flying off. A hasty getaway is particularly important given the Caspian's propensity to develop waterlogged wing feathers, as well as the possible threat of any nearby gulls giving chase to steal the fresh kill. A skilled aerialist, this species may fly dozens of miles away from coastlines while foraging, and its sleek and tapered silhouette allows for great deftness of reaction and rapidity of flight.

MIGRATE? Yes.

NESTING: Colonial nester, usually on islands (to offset the risk of mammalian predation). A shallow scrape is lined with debris and twigs. Usually less than 1 ft. across.

EGGS: Light brown or blue with dark mottling and spotting. Length of 2 ½ in. Total of 1-3.

FEEDER BEHAVIOR: Does not visit feeders.

COMPARE TO SIMILAR SPECIES: Long, distinctive bill characteristic of terns, in addition to bright orange bill coloration and streamlined head profile, quickly distinguish from gulls. Among terns, only the Royal Tern is of similarly large size, but is limited to oceanic coastlines. The Royal lacks the Caspian's perennially dark underwing feathers at the tips, as well as its entirely dark head cap in late summer through winter.

DID YOU KNOW? The Caspian Tern is the world's largest tern, and is regularly found on every continent with the exceptions of South America and Antarctica.

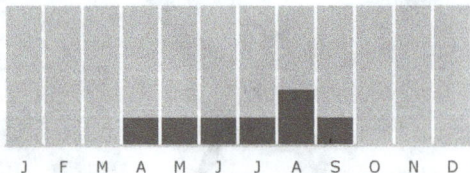

J F M A M J J A S O N D

Nonbreeding adult (Notice washed-out coloration of head cap) at top,
Breeding adult scanning water at bottom.

Breeding male at top,
Female with ducklings at bottom.

② **WOOD DUCK.** *Aix sponsa.*

SIZE: 20 in.

HABITAT: Wetlands and small waterways.

WILD DIET: Nuts, seeds, and berries; also, some aquatic invertebrates and insects.

BEHAVIOR: Forages by dabbling in the shallows or by slowly, adroitly walking on land. Tends to prefer sheltered habitats that offer plenty of shelter from predators, such as large raptors. Like other dabbling ducks which ply their trade in secluded wetlands, this species is flushed easily by human activity.

MIGRATE? Yes.

NESTING: Cavity nester. Natural hollows of mature trees (near water) are usually selected, often dozens of feet off the ground. The entry hole may be as small as 4-6 in. in diameter, but this species can adapt to a variety of cavity sizes. Lined with ample feathers.

EGGS: White to off-white. Length of 2 in. Total of 7-17, with 1-2 broods.

FEEDER BEHAVIOR: Does not visit feeders, but uses nest boxes.

COMPARE TO SIMILAR SPECIES: Male is very distinctive in breeding plumage. Nonbreeding and eclipse (molting, occurs during summer) males have washed-out coloration, and usually no green on head. Meanwhile, females have a noticeable white eye patch which extends toward the back of the head.

DID YOU KNOW? As with other duck species, male Wood Ducks are known as drakes, and females as hens. All ducks undergo full molts of their flight feathers during the warmer months, which render them completely flightless for several weeks. In order to better avoid predation and other perceived threats, dabbling ducks such as the Wood Duck tend to situate themselves in the densely vegetated corners of marshes for this period, which provide ample cover. Accordingly, the more brightly colored drakes display a washed-out eclipse plumage during this time to provide better concealment.

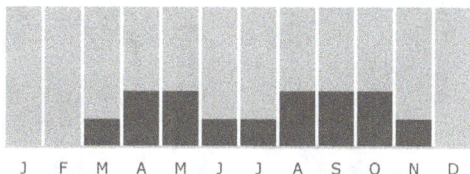

J F M A M J J A S O N D

③ **RING-BILLED GULL.** *Larus delawarensis.*

SIZE: 19 in.

HABITAT: Coastlines, wetlands, landfills, picnic areas.

WILD DIET: Insects, fish, worms, grains, rodents, garbage at landfills.

BEHAVIOR: Forages at the surface of water, in mudflats and tidal areas, at garbage dumps, and sometimes near urban habitation. Often seen milling about or orderly standing in large parking lots and on piers. Individuals tend to exhibit an uncanny degree of resourcefulness, with a highly varied diet and a well-adapted lifestyle to the modern Anthropocene. Individuals may regularly visit the dumpsters near picnic areas or fast-food restaurants, seeking out food scraps and even the small flying insects which gather overhead. In areas with higher degrees of human contact, Ring-billed Gulls have been known to approach humans for food, even nabbing unguarded morsels from outdoor benches and tables.

MIGRATE? Partially.

NESTING: Nests in groups of up to many thousands on sand, concrete, and rocky beaches. Little to no nest lining.

EGGS: Light blue-green to light brown, with dark splotching. Length of 2 ½ in. Total of 3.

FEEDER BEHAVIOR: Does not visit feeders.

COMPARE TO SIMILAR SPECIES: Most similar to Herring Gull. Note the Ring-billed's bright, yellow legs, contrasted with the pale, pink legs of the Herring Gull. Ring-billed Gulls are also smaller, more slight of build, and are most likely to have a sharply defined black ring near the end of the bill.

DID YOU KNOW? Ring-billed Gulls are able to accurately sense their magnetic bearings as soon as they are a few days old. This navigational aptitude allows them to accurately judge the correct direction for their migration routes.

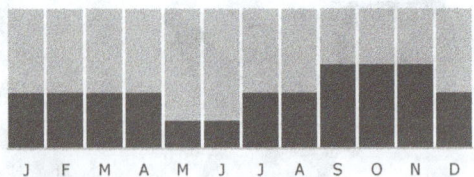

J F M A M J J A S O N D

Adult in breeding plumage at top (Photo by Mdf / CC BY-SA / Cropped),
Adult in nonbreeding plumage at bottom (Notice light, dirty streaking on head and neck).

Adult male at top,
Adult female at middle,
Juvenile at bottom.

① **NORTHERN HARRIER.** *Circus hudsonius.*

SIZE: 19 in.

HABITAT: Mostly open country, including fields, farmland, prairie, and open marshland. Breeds in wetlands.

WILD DIET: Small mammals (e.g., voles, mice, and shrews), small birds (e.g., sparrows), reptiles and amphibians, and occasionally large insects.

BEHAVIOR: Solitary glider over the ground with wings held in a V-shape, typically seeking out small rodent prey. Occasional quick, strong flaps allow the harrier to remain aloft as it circles and explores its feeding grounds. When movement is sighted, it will briefly contort its body as it enters a predatory dive. During migration—which, in fall, occurs much later than most other migrating raptors—harriers are a common sight in the skies, soaring with steady wingbeats and often holding their wings in a shallower V-shape than when hunting. During the winter, individuals flock together at nighttime roosts, which may be situated directly on the ground in fields.

MIGRATE? Partially.

NESTING: Nests on the ground in wetlands, usually concealed from view. Platform of reeds and twigs. Nearly 2 ft. across.

EGGS: Off-white to light blue. Length of 2 in. Total of 3-7.

FEEDER BEHAVIOR: Does not visit feeders.

COMPARE TO SIMILAR SPECIES: Owl-like facial features and dihedral (V-shaped) wing shape while gliding are most diagnostic for this species. In addition, each individual displays a prominent white rump, directly above the tail feathers.

DID YOU KNOW? Northern Harriers are polygynous breeders, meaning that each male mates with multiple females over the course of the breeding season. This consequently makes for a busy period of hunting in the late spring as hatchlings from each of the male's sired nests must be duly fed.

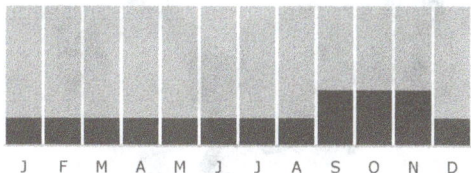

J F M A M J J A S O N D

67

⑤ AMERICAN CROW. *Corvus brachyrhynchos.*

SIZE: 19 in.

HABITAT: Nearly anywhere, but especially open woods.

WILD DIET: Nearly anything, including nuts and fruits, grains and seeds, eggs and hatchlings, insects and spiders, worms, mice, carrion, and garbage.

BEHAVIOR: Highly intelligent. Engages in sophisticated communication, problem-solving, and self-governing behavior in groups. Often observed in flocks, also known as murders (e.g., a murder of crows).

MIGRATE? No.

NESTING: Hidden in a fork near the trunk of a tree, and near the tree's apex. Cup-shaped, formed from twigs and lined with vegetation. Usually about 1 ft. wide and 6 in. deep.

EGGS: Shades of blue-green, with speckling. Length of 1 ½ in. Total of 3-6.

BIRD FEEDING TIPS

FEEDER DIET: Black-oil and hulled sunflower seeds, suet, oats, cracked corn, peanuts and peanut hearts, millet, milo, fruit. **FEEDER TYPES**: Ground, platforms. **FEEDER BEHAVIOR**: Large size may intimidate some birds upon arrival. Tends to have a large appetite, which proves problematic for some feeder setups, and may take excess food to store elsewhere.

COMPARE TO SIMILAR SPECIES: Most similar to Common Raven, but smaller. Smooth head and throat feathers, while tail is more fan-shaped than wedge-shaped when unfurled. Also, note the characteristic *caw, caw* calls which are familiar across much of the U.S.

DID YOU KNOW? Among many other examples of tool use, crows have taken discarded, still-lit cigarettes and rubbed them inside of their wings to kill parasites; sharpened sticks to poke between fence posts, so as to feed on hidden insects, seeds, and grains; and rewarded humans who set out food with shiny trinkets that they carried from nearby.

J F M A M J J A S O N D

Perching adult at top (Photo by Becky Matsubara / CC BY-SA / Cropped),
Flying adult at bottom.

Male at top,
Male and female at bottom.

① GREATER SCAUP (or BLUEBILL).
Aythya marila.

SIZE: 18 in.

HABITAT: Bays and coastlines of oceans and large lakes. Occasionally, a short distance offshore. Breeds in wetlands, mostly in Alaska.

WILD DIET: Aquatic invertebrates, insects, and aquatic vegetation.

BEHAVIOR: Often observed in very large groups somewhat near shore, which can reach sizes of hundreds or even thousands. Dives for food in water under 10 feet deep, but can dive up to 25 feet beneath the surface. These dives may last over a minute, and foraging is conducted by dragging its bill purposefully through the bottom substrate. May form mixed-species flocks with the similarly colored Lesser Scaup, as well as with the Canvasback and Redhead.

MIGRATE? Yes.

NESTING: Nests on the water or on next to the water's edge, using floating vegetation or tangled grasses, respectively. Typically takes the shape of a shallow bowl. About 1 ft. across.

EGGS: Gray to light olive. Length of 2 ½ in. Total of 6-13.

FEEDER BEHAVIOR: Does not visit feeders.

COMPARE TO SIMILAR SPECIES: Most similar to the slightly smaller Lesser Scaup. Greater Scaup males have tinges of green, rather than purple, in their dark head plumage, and may be brighter white on the sides of the belly. Both sexes of Greater have a smoothly rounded head crown, while the Lesser's tapers to a point near the rear of the crown.

DID YOU KNOW? Like most other ducks, Greater Scaups roost on the water, which can make them quite vulnerable to nocturnal owl attacks—particularly due to their conspicuously large flocks. However, the ducks can often sense an approaching owl by the vibrations its wing strokes make against the surface of the water, with many lookouts potentially offering greater security during a long winter's night.

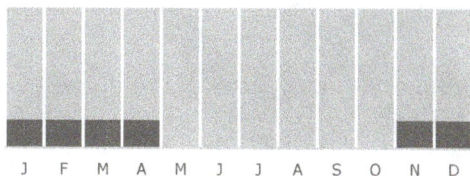

J F M A M J J A S O N D

71

② COMMON GOLDENEYE. *Bucephala clangula.*

SIZE: 18 in.

HABITAT: Bays and coastlines of oceans and large lakes, rivers. Breeds near smaller bodies of water or wetlands.

WILD DIET: Mostly aquatic invertebrates. Also aquatic vegetation, small fish and fish eggs, and insects.

BEHAVIOR: A diving duck, this species forages by gracefully diving beneath the surface in search of prey. During warmer winters, this species is known to remain farther north, so long as sufficient ice-free habitat remains. May outcompete other diving ducks for habitat and resources, and is thus seldom found in mixed-species flocks.

MIGRATE? Yes.

NESTING: Cavity nester, using natural or woodpecker-manufactured hollows in trees, as well as nest boxes. Often returns to the same nest. Lined with feathers, and less than 1 ft. across.

EGGS: Shades of light green to blue-green. Length of 2 ½ in. Total of 5-9.

FEEDER BEHAVIOR: Does not visit feeders, but uses nest boxes.

COMPARE TO SIMILAR SPECIES: Most similar to the more westerly, and less common, Barrow's Goldeneye. Common males possess diagonal, sloping white markings along the folded wing, while Barrow's males have smaller white spots. Common females have gold coloration on just the tip of the bill (rather than a larger portion or its entirety), and a bill which is roughly flush with the slope of the head.

DID YOU KNOW? When chicks first leave the nest, which may be several dozen feet above the ground, they jump out and tumble to the ground: like many other species of cavity-nesting ducks. Their light weight and heavy feathering protect against the impact, and—before long—the ducklings are following their mother to water in a grand display of the delicate beginnings of life.

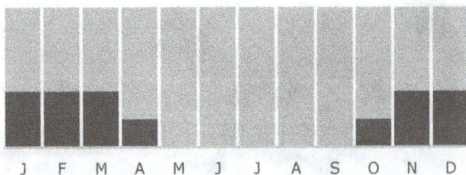

J F M A M J J A S O N D

Male at top,
Female at bottom.

Perching adult at top (Photo by Mosharaf Hossain / CC BY-SA / Cropped),
Flying adult at bottom (Photo by Andy Reago, Chrissy McClarren / CC BY-SA / Cropped).

① PEREGRINE FALCON. *Falco peregrinus.*

SIZE: 18 in.

HABITAT: Coastlines, mountains and valleys, and cities.

WILD DIET: Mostly medium-sized birds (e.g., pigeons, ducks, and gulls); also bats.

BEHAVIOR: Often watching for prey from an elevated perch or from high in the sky. Once prey is sighted, this bird enters a steep dive, reaching speeds of over 240 mph, culminating in a quick strike-and-kill. May also pursue prey from lower heights, flying up to 70 mph horizontally in pursuit: though cruising speeds are often just 30 to 40 mph. Individuals may periodically specialize in certain modes of hunting, depending on dietary needs and habitat characteristics. Some have been known to regularly soar high and dive upon Blue Jays, producing a puff of airborne feathers upon impact, while others have perched near inlets of bays, eagerly awaiting flocks of coots or ducks to unsuspectingly approach. Peregrines are increasingly taking up residence in urban environments, where they hunt pigeons and regularly nest on skyscraper ledges, the latter simulating its natural preference for cliffside nesting.

MIGRATE? Partially. Passing migrants sometimes observable in early spring and fall.

NESTING: Cliffside ledges. The topsoil is scraped away to form a shallow indentation. About 8 in. across.

EGGS: Off-white to red-brown, with splotchiness. Length of 2 in. Total of 2-4.

FEEDER BEHAVIOR: Does not visit feeders.

COMPARE TO SIMILAR SPECIES: Pointed, swept-back wings differentiate from other birds of prey, such as hawks or eagles. Among falconids, much larger than the Merlin and American Kestrel.

DID YOU KNOW? Like a guided missile, the Peregrine Falcon is able to make minute, controlled adjustments to the direction and camber of its dive to more accurately strike its moving targets. Aeronautical engineers have studied these characteristics for decades in order to understand the potential applications for aircraft, drones, and missiles. This is an example of *biomimicry*, wherein human engineering is modelled after materials or behaviors observed in the animal kingdom—which makes plenty of sense, considering the degree of specialization that each animal must possess to best exploit its well-honed ecological niche.

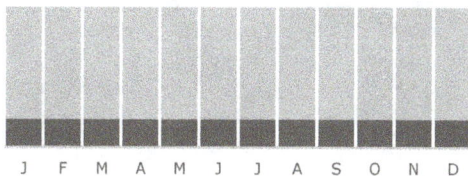

J F M A M J J A S O N D

(2) **RUFFED GROUSE.** *Bonasa umbellus.*

SIZE: 18 in.

HABITAT: Forests with plenty of thickets (i.e., successional woodland). Sometimes present on quiet roadsides.

WILD DIET: Wide variety of vegetation and fruits, sometimes insects.

BEHAVIOR: Furtively forages on the ground amid dense brush cover, making this species sometimes difficult to spot. During the winter, known to burrow into snowbanks. Populations tend to cycle over multi-year periods due to food availability and the length of winters. Most easily locatable by its wing-beating drumming behavior, which is used most frequently during mating and may be heard up to a half-mile away; this drumming is of a muted timbre, as if produced by hitting a drum repeatedly with a brush rather than with a wooden drumstick.

MIGRATE? No.

NESTING: Selects a location on the ground near a tree, log, or large rock. A shallow impression is scraped into leaf litter, which may be lined with twigs or other vegetation. About 6 in. across and 2-4 in. deep.

EGGS: White, sometimes with a reddish cast and/or red-brown speckling. Length of 1 ½ in. Total of 8-14.

FEEDER BEHAVIOR: Does not visit feeders.

COMPARE TO SIMILAR SPECIES: Spruce Grouse is black or darker brown, and resides in mature coniferous woods.

DID YOU KNOW? Ruffed Grouse populations have suffered one of the steepest declines of any North American bird species over the past thirty years. This is attributable, in part, to forest management practices which prioritize widescale tree-planting after the loss of tracts of mature woodland. However, this does not allow for woodland density to naturally regenerate over time, which forms transitional zones of thicket and is critical for species diversity.

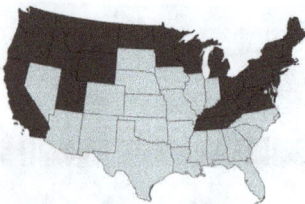

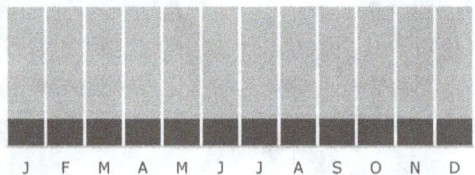

J F M A M J J A S O N D

Adult in typical habitat at top,
Adult drumming from elevated position at bottom.

Male at top,
Male and female at bottom.

② **HOODED MERGANSER.** *Lophodytes cucullatus.*

SIZE: 18 in.

HABITAT: Wetlands, ponds, small lakes and rivers. Occasionally, coastal bays.

WILD DIET: Mostly fish and aquatic invertebrates. Also, small amphibians, insects, and aquatic vegetation.

BEHAVIOR: This species typically congregates in small groups on protected bodies of water, irregularly diving beneath the surface to forage for prey. When diving, the merganser half-leaps from its floating position into the water, producing a clean entrance with minimal surface disturbance—which is important for maintaining its cover when hunting. This duck is able to change directions quickly while underwater, and even observe its surroundings in the most turbid of conditions. Like other mergansers, this species has minute serrations on the lining of its bill, which assist with grasping and securing underwater prey.

MIGRATE? Partially.

NESTING: Cavity nester, using natural or woodpecker-manufactured hollows in trees, as well as nest boxes. Lined with feathers. Entrance less than 6 in. wide.

EGGS: White to off-white, and somewhat spherical. Length of 2 in. Total of 7-13.

FEEDER BEHAVIOR: Does not visit feeders, but uses nest boxes.

COMPARE TO SIMILAR SPECIES: Males have a white head marking resembling that of the Bufflehead, but the rest of its markings are very different. Females may vaguely resemble other merganser species, but Hoodeds are much smaller and possess a more noticeable tuft at the rear of the head.

DID YOU KNOW? Hooded Mergansers have been observed repeatedly throughout the past decade in Dublin, Ireland, but it is likely that these are captive escapees and that they have not yet established a viable breeding population.

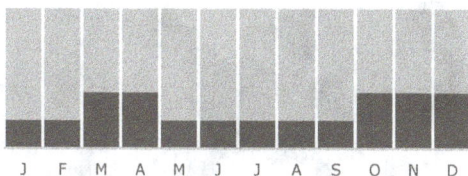

| J | F | M | A | M | J | J | A | S | O | N | D |

② PILEATED WOODPECKER. *Dryocopus pileatus.*

SIZE: 18 in.

HABITAT: Dense, mature woods. Sometimes, semi-open woods and wooded suburbs.

WILD DIET: Mostly insects (in particular, carpenter ants), also some nuts and fruits.

BEHAVIOR: Clings to tree bark while boring into the wood. Individuals may excavate deeply into the trunk, forming ovaline hollows recognizable long after the woodpecker has passed through. These forays are often intended to root out ant colonies; the woodpecker's long, extensible tongue is highly sensitive, and acts both as a tactile antenna and a dexterous tool for rooting out food sources (*See* Photo at bottom left). Occasionally forages at ground level. Likely sparse across its habitat, as individual breeding pairs aggressively defend a territory of several hundred acres from other conspecifics: with loud drilling often used as a signaling mechanism to potential rivals.

MIGRATE? No.

NESTING: Inside dead trees, where a round-entranced cavity is bored 1-2 ft. deep.

EGGS: Milky white with light spotting. Length of 1 ¼ in. Total of 3-5.

BIRD FEEDING TIPS

FEEDER DIET: Suet, black-oil and hulled sunflower seeds, peanuts, mealworms. **FEEDER TYPES**: Suet cages. **FEEDER BEHAVIOR**: Hammers its bill against the suet to dislodge bite-size pieces. Other birds may initially fly away if startled by its arrival.

COMPARE TO SIMILAR SPECIES: Size and distinctive head markings contrast with those of other woodpeckers.

DID YOU KNOW? Pileated Woodpeckers rarely reuse the same nest cavity. This allows many other cavity-nesting birds, many of which are not able to drill their own cavities, to use the hole for nests in future years.

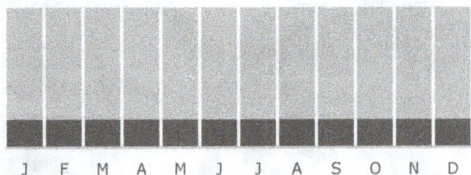

J F M A M J J A S O N D

Adults at top and bottom.

Adults at top and bottom.

① **GREEN HERON.** *Butorides virescens.*

SIZE: 17 in.

HABITAT: Wetlands and ponds, sometimes edges of reservoirs and small lakes.

WILD DIET: Mainly small fish. Also, frogs, insects and spiders, small rodents, and aquatic invertebrates.

BEHAVIOR: A solitary hunter at dusk and dawn, usually remaining somewhat secretive during the day. This species is often observed perched motionless on the edge of the water or in the shallows, waiting for prey to approach. Individuals may also rest aboveground in dense tangles of branches. Suburbanites very occasionally observe these birds flying between foraging locations, with somewhat quick, labored wingbeats, head tucked back, and legs outstretched behind.

MIGRATE? Yes.

NESTING: Hidden amid dense cover in the crotch of a tree, usually near wetland habitat. Twigs are used to weave a sturdy bowl. About 1 ft. in diameter.

EGGS: Light blue-green. Length of 1 ½ in. Total of 2-5, occasionally with a second brood.

FEEDER BEHAVIOR: Does not visit feeders.

COMPARE TO SIMILAR SPECIES: Dark green back and head, chestnut-colored chest, yellow legs, and partially yellow bill distinguish from other herons and bitterns. Juveniles are buffier all over, with a dark head crown.

DID YOU KNOW? The Green Heron is known for exhibiting remarkable feats of intelligence. It sometimes bait-fishes by finding a piece of bread, an insect, or a colorful object to drop on the water's surface; fish are attracted to the decoy and immediately snatched by the heron. Locations where Green Herons have used bread are also frequented by fishermen; consequently, scientists believe that these clever birds may have learned to bait-fish by direct observation of humans.

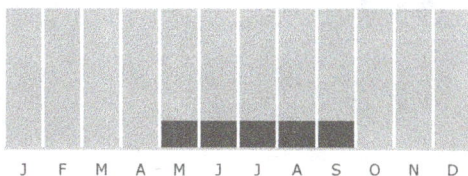

J F M A M J J A S O N D

83

① LESSER SCAUP (or LITTLE BLUEBILL).
Aythya affinis.

SIZE: 17 in.

HABITAT: Mostly large lakes (especially in bays), but also smaller bodies of water. Breeds in wetlands, usually in Canada or Alaska, as well as in the northwest-central U.S.

WILD DIET: Aquatic invertebrates, also insects and aquatic vegetation.

BEHAVIOR: Usually dives for food in water less than 10 feet deep, but can dive up to 25 feet beneath the surface. These dives may last over a minute, and foraging is conducted by dragging its bill purposefully through the substrate. May be found in medium to large flocks, sometimes with the similarly colored Greater Scaup, as well as the Canvasback or Redhead.

MIGRATE? Yes.

NESTING: Nests on the water or on next to the water's edge, using floating vegetation or tangled grasses, respectively. Typically takes the shape of a shallow bowl.

EGGS: Light brown to olive. Length of 2 - 2 ½ in. Total of 6-13.

FEEDER BEHAVIOR: Does not visit feeders.

COMPARE TO SIMILAR SPECIES: Most similar to the slightly larger Greater Scaup. Greater Scaup males have tinges of green, rather than purple, in their dark head plumage, and may be brighter white on the sides of the belly. Both sexes of Greater have a smoothly rounded head crown, while the Lesser's tapers to a point near the rear of the crown.

DID YOU KNOW? Lesser and Greater Scaups, as well as some other diving duck species in the Great Lakes, have been adversely affected by the rapid spread of the invasive zebra mussel. This mollusk from eastern Europe is known to act as a biological sponge for many toxins, such as selenium. Scaups with a diet high in zebra mussels—and, consequently, selenium—have struggled with infertility, as well as other issues.

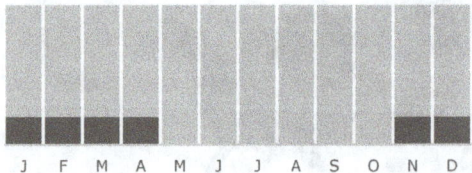

J F M A M J J A S O N D

Male at top,
Female at bottom.

Close-up of male at top,
Two males with female at bottom.

① **RING-NECKED DUCK.** *Aythya collaris.*

SIZE: 17 in.

HABITAT: Wetlands and shallow lakes, ponds. Breeds in wetlands.

WILD DIET: Mostly aquatic vegetation, also aquatic invertebrates and insects.

BEHAVIOR: This species favors the shallows—fully diving beneath the surface as it forages throughout the water column. Compared to many of the dabbling ducks which share their shallow, aquatic habitats, these brief dives enable the Ring-necked Duck to reach vegetation otherwise out of reach for many other species. Sometimes flocks in very large groups, but also may be found in small groups of under a dozen. Mature individuals seem to prefer vegetation to a mixed, omnivorous diet.

MIGRATE? Yes.

NESTING: Nests directly on the water, forming a loose, makeshift bowl of twigs, stems, and grasses atop floating mats of vegetation. About 1 - 1 ½ ft. across.

EGGS: Light brown. Length of 2 in. Total of 6-12.

FEEDER BEHAVIOR: Does not visit feeders.

COMPARE TO SIMILAR SPECIES: Most similar to the Greater and Lesser Scaup (which, it must be noted, tend to frequent larger bodies of water, such as bays), but male's feathery tuft atop the crown, black back, white markings up the side of the chest, and ring across bill are distinctive. Females are best identified by a light ring across the bill and a light eye-ring.

DID YOU KNOW? The Ring-necked Duck is named for the scarcely visible reddish-brown ring around the neck of males; this is typically only observable upon careful inspection at a close distance. In the early days of identification, observers would fire upon birds with shotguns and directly approach any fallen individuals—making finer details, such as the ring about this species' neck, much more visible. With binoculars not widely available before the late 1800s, this was the only manner by which most naturalists could accurately identify many of the birds they encountered.

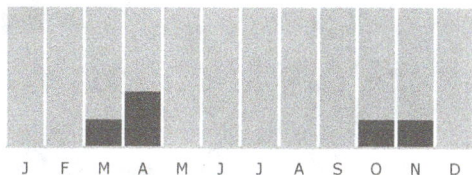

J F M A M J J A S O N D

② **COOPER'S HAWK.** *Accipiter cooperii.*

SIZE: 16 in.

HABITAT: Dense or open woods, suburbs.

WILD DIET: Mostly medium-sized birds (e.g., doves, robins, and jays), but also small rodents.

BEHAVIOR: Accustomed to deftly flying through cluttered woodland in search of prey. When pursuing its quarry, individuals will hopscotch among concealed perches before briskly swooping at all manner of angles to secure its catch. Its relatively short wings are extremely well adapted for this agile, close-quarters maneuvering, rather than the long gliding favored by many hawks of open country.

MIGRATE? Partially.

NESTING: Situated in large trees, 25-60 ft. above the ground. Platform composed of sticks, with small indentation in the center for eggs. About 2 ft. across and 1 ft. deep.

EGGS: Very light blue. Length of 2 in. Total of 3-5.

FEEDER BEHAVIOR: Often hunts at feeders, particularly if seed is present on the ground (so as to attract ground-feeding prey birds). After a sequence of attacks, it may take several days for feeder activity to fully return to previous levels.

COMPARE TO SIMILAR SPECIES: Longer tail, head-cap markings, coloration, and habitat selection usually differentiate from Red-tailed and Red-shouldered Hawks. Well-defined dark cap on top of head, as well as often larger size, differentiate adults from adult Sharp-shinned Hawks. Larger size and more defined, mocha-brown markings on chest differentiate juveniles from juvenile Sharp-shinned Hawks.

DID YOU KNOW? Given their penchant for weaving among trees beneath the forest canopy, as many as one-third of all individuals suffer fractures of bones in the chest at some point in their lives, though these wounds tend to recalcify in time.

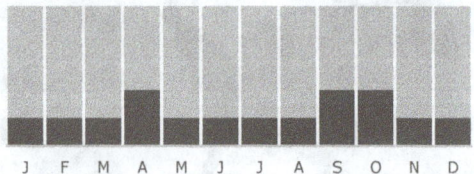

J F M A M J J A S O N D

Adult at top,
Juvenile at bottom (Photo by Tony Alter / CC BY-SA / Cropped).

Male at top (Photo by Mike Pazzani / CC BY-SA / Cropped),
Females at bottom.

① **BUFFLEHEAD.** *Bucephala albeola.*

SIZE: 14 in.

HABITAT: Harbors and bays of oceans, lakes, and reservoirs. May visit smaller bodies of water during migration, and especially during breeding season.

WILD DIET: Almost entirely aquatic invertebrates and insects.

BEHAVIOR: The smallest diving duck in North America, this species dives repeatedly below the surface for intervals of less than a half-minute, and to depths of up to 20 feet. It must take these foraging dives persistently throughout the day in order to sustain its unusually high metabolism. Like other diving ducks, this species is not usually observed walking on land, with the feet set behind each individual's center of mass to best allow for efficient underwater paddling. Furthermore, its diminutive size is specifically adapted to fill a unique ecological niche. While individuals forage in habitats frequented by other diving ducks, they nest almost entirely in cavities left by Northern Flickers, rather than the larger hollows left by Pileated Woodpeckers (which are subject to fierce competition from other, larger cavity-nesting ducks).

MIGRATE? Yes.

NESTING: Breeds in wooded areas near lakes and ponds. Nests in cavities left by Northern Flickers, or in nest boxes. Lined with feathers. Entrance usually less than 4 in. wide.

EGGS: Shiny, milky white. Length of 2 in. Total of 6-12.

FEEDER BEHAVIOR: Does not visit feeders, but sometimes uses nest boxes.

COMPARE TO SIMILAR SPECIES: White chest and belly distinguish males from Hooded Merganser males, and females have a distinctive white mark behind the eye.

DID YOU KNOW? The seemingly large head of this duck led early observers to give it the name of "buffalo head," the portmanteau of which remains this species' common name today. Similarly, the genus name is derived from the Ancient Greek *Bucephalus*, or "ox-headed," which was also the given name of Alexander the Great's valorous, well-renowned warhorse.

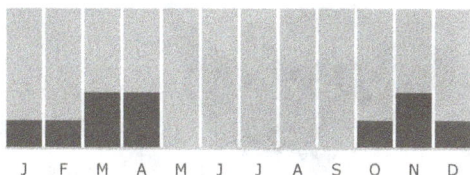

J F M A M J J A S O N D

① GREEN-WINGED TEAL. *Anas carolinensis.*

SIZE: 14 in.

HABITAT: Wetlands, ponds, mudflats, and sometimes agricultural fields.

WILD DIET: Mostly aquatic vegetation, also agricultural waste grains and aquatic invertebrates.

BEHAVIOR: A dabbling duck, this species periodically upends itself as it forages just below the water's surface, though mudflats are another favored foraging site. The Green-winged Teal is the smallest dabbling duck in North America, and is able to adapt to a variety of wetland habitats.

MIGRATE? Yes.

NESTING: Selects a site near, but not usually adjacent to, wetlands. A shallow, small depression is scraped into the grass and lined with twigs, grasses, and feathers. About 6 in. across.

EGGS: Off-white. Length of 2 in. Total of 7-12.

FEEDER BEHAVIOR: Does not visit feeders.

COMPARE TO SIMILAR SPECIES: Male is best identified by its horizontal green facial patch and silvery body. Females lack pale coloration at the base of the bill, which is notably found in female Blue-winged Teals. Females also have a pale, white stripe beneath the tail. Wholly dark-gray bill and diminutive size help to differentiate females from those of other, larger species (such as the common Mallard).

DID YOU KNOW? The story of the Green-winged Teal is often all about the debates surrounding its subspecies. The Eurasian Teal is considered by some to be a separate species entirely, and by others to be conspecific; rare vagrants are sometimes observed on the Atlantic coast, with males best identified by their horizontal white marking along the upper folded wing. The Aleutian Islands subspecies, meanwhile, is unusual in that it has adapted to live year-round in its habitat, despite the inhospitable winter conditions; some of these birds feed on beaches during winter, possibly mimicking a natural preference for mudflats.

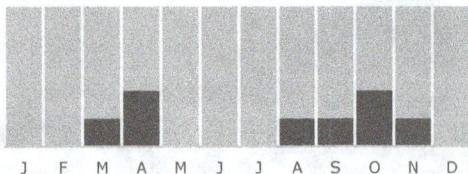

J F M A M J J A S O N D

Male at top,
Female at bottom (Photo by Mike Pazzani / CC BY-SA).

Breeding adults at top,
Nonbreeding adult at bottom.

① HORNED GREBE. *Podiceps auritus.*

SIZE: 14 in.

HABITAT: Coastlines of oceans, lakes, and reservoirs. Occasionally, ponds and rivers. In Vermont, most common at Lake Champlain.

WILD DIET: Aquatic invertebrates, small fish, and insects.

BEHAVIOR: Like other grebes, this species is known for its extraordinary aptitude for swimming and diving—owing to large, webbed feet located well behind the center of gravity. Consequently, individuals are most often observed on the water, and rarely on land. May launch submerged attacks on small ducks during the breeding season to defend its territory. Found by itself or in very small groups in both the shallows and a few hundred yards offshore in open water, at depths of up to 50 to 80 feet.

MIGRATE? Yes.

NESTING: Anchored to floating aquatic vegetation, and takes the approximate shape of a platform. Constructed of twigs and stems. Less than 8 in. wide.

EGGS: Off-white to brown. Length of 1 ½ - 2 in. Total of 3-6, occasionally with a second brood.

FEEDER BEHAVIOR: Does not visit feeders.

COMPARE TO SIMILAR SPECIES: Breeding adults are highly distinctive. Nonbreeding adults are slightly larger than the similar nonbreeding Eared Grebe, which is less common and more westerly in its range; additional differences include the Horned's oblong (rather than somewhat round or square) head, and more complete white coloration along the side of the head and neck.

DID YOU KNOW? The introduction of certain fish species for sport, such as rainbow trout (also known as steelhead) across North America, has led to diminishing food supplies for grebes, which have suffered declines in the past half-century. Grebes are generally also sensitive to salinity and toxin levels in their habitats, which can affect the availability of food and nesting materials.

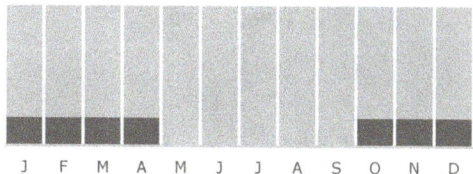

J F M A M J J A S O N D

① **PIED-BILLED GREBE.** *Podilymbus podiceps.*

SIZE: 14 in.

HABITAT: Wetlands, ponds, lakes, and calmer sections of rivers.

WILD DIET: Mostly crustaceans and small fish (up to 6 in. long). Also, other aquatic invertebrates, insects, and amphibians.

BEHAVIOR: Active divers, grebes are known for their exceptional maneuverability while swimming underwater—on account of large, webbed feet located behind the center of gravity. As a result of this adaptation, individuals tend to be quite ungainly on land and are almost always observed in the water. With graceful, arced leaps, these birds frequently dive below the surface and can reach depths of up to 50 feet repeatedly throughout the day. When surfacing with a small fish, the grebe tosses and spins the catch in its bill, before swallowing it headfirst. Often found in small groups or by themselves, scattered across the surface of the water.

MIGRATE? Yes.

NESTING: Anchored to floating aquatic vegetation, and takes the approximate shape of a platform. Constructed of twigs and stems. Less than 6 in. wide.

EGGS: White. Length of 1 ½ - 2 in. Total of 3-8, sometimes with a second brood.

FEEDER BEHAVIOR: Does not visit feeders.

COMPARE TO SIMILAR SPECIES: Very small size among the waterfowl, and distinctively small and stubby bill relative to other species. The similarly sized, less common Horned Grebe has a noticeably more pointed bill, and features differing coloration (e.g., black and gold head with reddish body in breeding months, partially white head and neck with dark gray body in nonbreeding months).

DID YOU KNOW? Grebes, including the Pied-billed, are well-known for consuming their own feathers, which may help with the following: protecting the stomach from indigestible bones or shells, preventing these items from passing to the intestines, or allowing for these indigestible items to be more easily packaged as pellets for regurgitation. In some grebes, the stomach has been observed to be up to half-full with feathered contents.

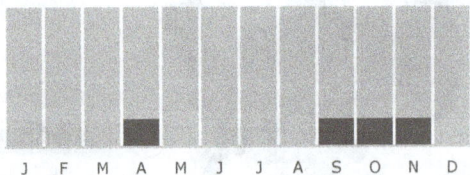

J F M A M J J A S O N D

Breeding adult with juvenile at top,
Nonbreeding adult at bottom.

Adult at top,
Adults in flight at bottom.

③ ROCK DOVE (or ROCK PIGEON).
Columba livia.

SIZE: 13 in.

HABITAT: Urban areas and highway overpasses. Sometimes, farmland: particularly near grain silos.

WILD DIET: Grains, seeds, berries, and garbage.

BEHAVIOR: Forages on the ground, often in flocks of at least several dozen. Also loiters in parks if there is a consistent source of human-supplied food. While walking along, this species repeatedly nods its head forward, which provides a steadier field of vision by counterbalancing its choppy gait. Large flocks are often observed perched on telephone wires, along ledges of buildings, or atop billboards.

MIGRATE? No.

NESTING: In urban areas, nests in crevices or on ledges of buildings, particularly where there is some overhead shelter. Small platform, constructed with sticks and vegetation. Over time, may grow in size with the accumulated feces of past nesting generations.

EGGS: White. Length of 1 ½ in. Total of 2. Usually raises 3-4 broods each year, but may raise up to 6.

BIRD FEEDING TIPS

FEEDER DIET: Black-oil and hulled sunflower seeds, cracked corn, peanut hearts, millet, safflower seed. **FEEDER TYPES**: Ground, platforms, hoppers. **FEEDER BEHAVIOR**: Most likely to visit if feeders are situated near urban centers, bridges, or overpasses.

COMPARE TO SIMILAR SPECIES: Similar in shape and silhouette to Mourning Dove, but note clear difference in coloration and markings.

DID YOU KNOW? Due to their characteristic homing abilities, domesticated pigeons have long been used to convey messages to distant locations. Rock Doves, in particular, have been used to carry such things as postal messages and wartime communications over distances spanning hundreds—and even thousands—of miles.

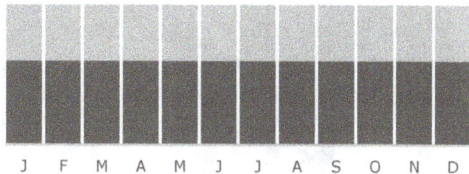

J F M A M J J A S O N D

① GREATER YELLOWLEGS. *Tringa melanoleuca.*

SIZE: 13 in.

HABITAT: Wetlands, mudflats, flooded fields; also, edges of streams, ponds, reservoirs, lakes.

WILD DIET: Aquatic insects and invertebrates, sometimes fish and small frogs.

BEHAVIOR: Usually observed foraging solitarily, with a slight preference for deeper portions of shallows compared to other shorebirds. Wades through the water or walks across mudflats with a peculiar, high-stepping motion. Known for striking its prey with a quick downward peck or by repeated probing motions: particularly when foraging in more turbid, or opaque, waters. Rather unusually for a shorebird, males may be observed standing sentry over their nesting territories from elevated positions in the treetops, most often during the breeding season.

MIGRATE? Yes.

NESTING: Selects a concealed location amid the dense vegetation at the edges of wetlands. Digs a light scrape in the moss or soil. Up to 6 in. across.

EGGS: Light brown with heavy dark mottling. Length of 2 in. Total of 3-4.

FEEDER BEHAVIOR: Does not visit feeders.

COMPARE TO SIMILAR SPECIES: Large size and conspicuous, bright yellow legs distinguish from most other shorebird species. Lesser Yellowlegs is very similar, but stands a few inches shorter, and has a bill approximately the length of its head (compared to that of the Greater, which is at least one-and-a-half times the length of its head). Also, the bill of the Greater is slightly upturned at the end, though this can be difficult to spot in the field.

DID YOU KNOW? Despite its remarkable similarity with the Lesser Yellowlegs, this species is actually more closely related to the gray-legged Willet. All three species are members of the *Tringa* genus, which was named for an antiquitous shorebird originally described by the Greek polymath Aristotle.

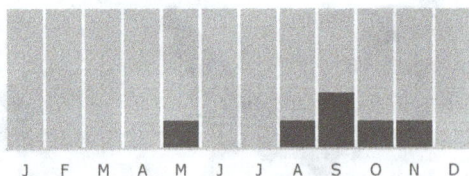

J F M A M J J A S O N D

Breeding adult at top,
Nonbreeding adult at bottom.

Male at top,
Female at bottom (Notice presence of chestnut breast coloration).

② **BELTED KINGFISHER.** *Megaceryle alcyon.*

SIZE: 13 in.

HABITAT: Variety of bodies of water, including bays, lakes, rivers, and ponds. Prefers to hunt over calm, clearer water whenever available.

WILD DIET: Mostly small fish (e.g., trout, perch, sunfish, sticklebacks), sometimes crayfish, snails, amphibians, insects, and small mammals.

BEHAVIOR: This species is most often found on the fringes of local lakes, ponds, and streams: perched atop a post, branch, or wire overlooking the water. When prey is spotted, the kingfisher flies near the targeted location, briefly hovers momentarily on flapping wings, and plunge-dives bill-first to collect its meal. The catch is then consumed headfirst from a nearby perch. As the kingfisher flies about its habitat, it commonly emits a series of characteristic, rattling calls, which provide a telltale indicator of its nearby presence. A group of this species is accordingly known as a rattle or kerfuffle (e.g., a kerfuffle of kingfishers).

MIGRATE? Mostly.

NESTING: Digs a long, hidden burrow into a vertical or steeply sloped earthen bank. About 3-8 ft. deep with an enlarged, elevated nest chamber at the terminus.

EGGS: Bright white. Length of 1 ½ in. Total of 4-8, sometimes with a second brood.

FEEDER BEHAVIOR: Does not visit feeders.

COMPARE TO SIMILAR SPECIES: Very distinctive, with few birds resembling this species.

DID YOU KNOW? The tricks of the Belted Kingfisher's trade are carefully guarded and passed from generation to generation. Parents teach their young to hunt by dropping dead prey fish in the water for retrieval, allowing the young an opportunity to wet their bills before heading off on their own.

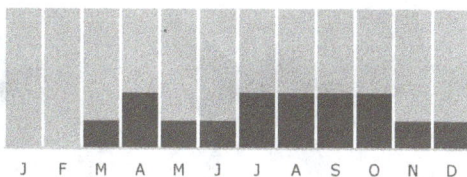

J F M A M J J A S O N D

④ **COMMON GRACKLE.** *Quiscalus quiscula.*

SIZE: 12 in.
HABITAT: Open woods, wetlands, fields, and suburbs.
WILD DIET: Seeds, grains, insects and spiders, frogs, eggs, mice, and small birds.
BEHAVIOR: Frequently forages across lawns and fields, and perches in shrubs or atop marsh grasses. Roosts high in trees. When flying in search of another location to scavenge, this species may emit a deep *chek* sound; the long, flowing tail with a diamond-like extension is characteristic of this species and highly recognizable.
MIGRATE? Yes.
NESTING: In conifers, well above the ground. Often near wetland habitats. Cup-shaped, constructed of grasses and twigs. Up to 12 in. across, and 8 in. tall.
EGGS: Shades of blue or blue-green, with dark mottling. Length of 1 in. Total of 3-6, occasionally with a second brood.

BIRD FEEDING TIPS

FEEDER DIET: Black-oil and hulled sunflower seeds, suet, mealworms, safflower seed, cracked corn, peanuts and peanut hearts, oats, millet, milo, fruit. **FEEDER TYPES:** Ground, platforms, hoppers. **FEEDER BEHAVIOR:** Can dominate feeders due to their size and attitudes. Often observed foraging on ground, or briefly perching on bark to feed on suet.

COMPARE TO SIMILAR SPECIES: Long tail with diamond-like attachment is largely distinctive among blackbirds of this size. In addition, the European Starling is smaller, has somewhat different markings, and lacks a relatively long tail.

DID YOU KNOW? The flocking tendency and resourcefulness of this species, along with its preference for seeds and grains, has resulted in millions of dollars' worth of damage to agricultural crops, especially corn.

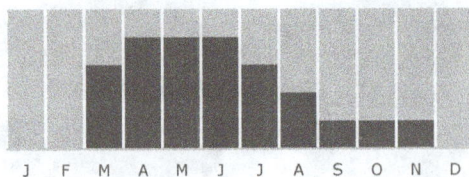

J F M A M J J A S O N D

Male at top,
Female at bottom (Photo by Bob Peterson / CC BY-SA / Cropped).

Adult at left,
Juvenile at right.

① SHARP-SHINNED HAWK. *Accipiter striatus.*

SIZE: 12 in.

HABITAT: Dense woods, sometimes wooded suburbs.

WILD DIET: Mostly small to medium-sized songbirds. Rarely, small rodents.

BEHAVIOR: Selects hidden perches at a variety of heights, ambushing prey with quick and stealthy approaches. Often flies nimbly through dense thickets and forest understories when hunting, requiring split-second reflexes and precise, acrobatic movements. As such, this hawk is a member of the accipiters (along with the closely related Cooper's Hawk), which tend to feature short, rounded wings and long, rudder-like tails as express adaptations for this hunting technique.

MIGRATE? Partially.

NESTING: Usually in conifers, well above the ground. Near the top of tree, but beneath the forest canopy. Platform-shaped and constructed with twigs. About 18 in. across and 4 in. deep.

EGGS: Off-white, with variety of bright splotches. Length of 1 ½ in. Total of 4-6.

FEEDER BEHAVIOR: Sometimes hunts at feeders, but less frequently than the Cooper's Hawk.

COMPARE TO SIMILAR SPECIES: Adults are superficially similar to the Cooper's Hawk, but smaller size, lack of a *separated* dark cap on head, and habitat choice are often helpful differences. Juveniles are separated from juvenile Cooper's by less-defined, splotchier, and tawnier chest markings.

DID YOU KNOW? Though one of the more secretive hawks found in North America, this species spectacularly travels en masse during migration, sometimes even overwhelming experienced hawk-watchers. As many as 10,000 individuals have been counted in a single day in some locations—the most productive of which tend to be situated along prominent coastlines or mountain ridges.

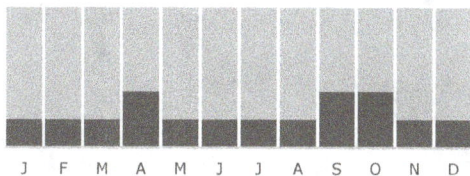

J F M A M J J A S O N D

107

② NORTHERN FLICKER. *Colaptes auratus.*

SIZE: 12 in.

HABITAT: Open woods, fields, and suburbs.

WILD DIET: Mostly insects and spiders (in particular, ants). Also, seeds and berries.

BEHAVIOR: These uniquely patterned woodpeckers are the only species of their kind which routinely feeds on the ground. Ant hills are often sought, and this species' long, nimble tongue is able to extend several inches from its bill to collect larvae and mature ants alike. If present in agricultural pastures, this bird may also hammer apart cow dung in order to feast on any insects present inside.

MIGRATE? Mostly. In the winter, more likely to be found in the southern half of the state.

NESTING: Excavated holes in dead tree trunks or large branches. May be reused from other species. Exterior hole is about 3-4 in. in diameter, and cavity is over 1 ft. deep.

EGGS: White. Length of 1 in. Total of 5-6, sometimes with a second brood.

BIRD FEEDING TIPS

FEEDER DIET: Suet, black-oil and hulled sunflower seeds, safflower seed, cracked corn, peanuts and peanut hearts, millet. **FEEDER TYPES**: Suet cages, ground, platforms, hoppers. **FEEDER BEHAVIOR**: Less common at feeders, but usually observed consuming suet from a cage, or scavenging on the ground.

COMPARE TO SIMILAR SPECIES: Coloration and spotted patterning are distinctive among woodpeckers. Much stouter, thicker neck than those of doves or robins.

DID YOU KNOW? During the breeding season, dueling males may engage in a bill-sparring match which roughly resembles the Olympic sport of fencing. The prospective female watches from a safe distance—awaiting the winner and soon-to-be mate.

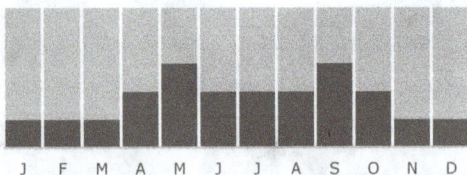

J F M A M J J A S O N D

Adults at top and bottom.

Breeding adult at top,
Nonbreeding adult at bottom.

① LESSER YELLOWLEGS. *Tringa flavipes.*

SIZE: 12 in.

HABITAT: Wetlands, mudflats, flooded fields; also, edges of streams, ponds, reservoirs, and lakes.

WILD DIET: Aquatic insects and invertebrates, sometimes fish and small frogs.

BEHAVIOR: Stalks through the shallows of its wetland habitat, occasionally increasing pace or pecking beneath the surface when prey is spotted. Like the Greater Yellowlegs, it also walks with a high-stepping gait and may wade up to its chest while foraging. This allows for individuals to exploit sections of wetland unsuitable for smaller shorebirds, such as Spotted or Least Sandpipers. When foraging, usually present by itself or in very small, scattered numbers. Hatchlings are precocious, leaving the nest within hours and effectively presenting a model of self-sufficiency.

MIGRATE? Yes.

NESTING: Well-concealed locations in the vicinity of its typical wetland habitat, often amid dense vegetation or debris. Digs a light scrape in the moss or soil. About 3-4 in. across.

EGGS: Light brown with heavy dark mottling. Length of 1 ½ - 2 in. Total of 3-4.

FEEDER BEHAVIOR: Does not visit feeders.

COMPARE TO SIMILAR SPECIES: Medium-large size and conspicuous, bright yellow legs distinguish from most other shorebird species. Greater Yellowlegs is very similar, but stands a few inches taller and has a bill at least one-and-a-half times the length of its head (compared to that of the Lesser, which is about the length of its head).

DID YOU KNOW? When flushed, this wary shorebird usually gives a one- or two-note squeaking call, rather than the more forceful three- or four-note call of the Greater Yellowlegs. To better recall this difference, consider that the Lesser Yellowlegs gives a "lesser" number of notes.

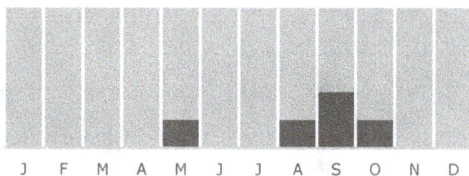

J F M A M J J A S O N D

⑤ MOURNING DOVE. *Zenaida macroura.*

SIZE: 12 in.

HABITAT: Open woods, fields, suburbs, roadsides.

WILD DIET: Various seeds.

BEHAVIOR: Often observed perching on wires, fences, roofs, and in trees, while repeatedly *hooing* with its signature, melancholy call. Pecks for food on the ground, and is not an overly picky eater. To accompany its voracious appetite for seeds, this species swallows fine rocks or sands to aid in digestion. Occasionally may be observed sunning itself on the ground, with wings and tail splayed out.

MIGRATE? Partially.

NESTING: Hidden among tree branches, in shrubs, on the ground, or in artificial objects such as eaves and gutters. Cup-shaped, and constructed with conifer needles, grasses, and small sticks. About 8 in. across.

EGGS: White. Length of 1 in. Total of 2. Usually raises 2-3 broods each year, but may raise up to 6.

BIRD FEEDING TIPS

FEEDER DIET: Black-oil and hulled sunflower seeds, safflower seed, cracked corn, peanut hearts, millet, oats, nyjer, milo. **FEEDER TYPES**: Ground, platforms, hoppers. **FEEDER BEHAVIOR**: May rest or forage beneath feeders. Common prey for feeder-raiding Cooper's Hawks, and sometimes Sharp-shinned or even Red-shouldered Hawks.

COMPARE TO SIMILAR SPECIES: Much paler than Rock Doves, and usually found in less urban areas. Tapered, feathered tails are easily observable when perching, which are very different from the more rectangular tails of Sharp-shinned Hawks and American Kestrels, not to mention many other visual differences.

DID YOU KNOW? Occasionally called turtle doves, these birds are anything but slow in flight—reaching speeds of up to 55 mph as they whistle through the air.

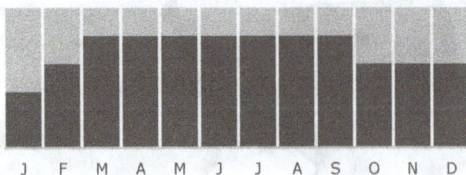

J F M A M J J A S O N D

Adult on ground at top,
Adult perched on wire at bottom (Photo by Heide Couch / CC BY-SA / Cropped).

Adults at top and bottom.

(1) **WILSON'S SNIPE.** *Gallinago delicata.*

SIZE: 11 in.

HABITAT: Wetlands, flooded fields, and ponds, usually with patches of dense vegetation.

WILD DIET: Insects and insect larvae, sometimes aquatic invertebrates.

BEHAVIOR: Pokes and probes its bill into mudflats and in shallow water while foraging. In part, this species is less commonly observed due to its camouflaging markings and penchant for concealing itself amid fallen logs and patches of vegetation. Sizable chest muscles allow for powerful wing strokes, which allow this rather portly bird to reach airspeeds of up to 65 mph—frequently resulting in a distinctive buzzing or winnowing sound from its feathers.

MIGRATE? Yes.

NESTING: Selects a concealed location adjacent to wetland shallows. A bowl-like impression is made in the soil or mud, and lined with woven reeds. About 6 in. across.

EGGS: Yellow-brown to creamy brown, with dark, cloudy mottling. Length of 1 ½ in. Total of 3-4.

FEEDER BEHAVIOR: Does not visit feeders.

COMPARE TO SIMILAR SPECIES: Solid brown stripe above pale eyeline on head, bold and dark patterning across body, and squat stature help to separate this species from the American Woodcock, which has a golden chest and different facial markings. Other similar species include the taller, leaner, less boldly patterned dowitchers (which sweep their bills back and forth while feeding).

DID YOU KNOW? This species is named for the early-1800s Scottish-American ornithologist Alexander Wilson, for whom the following species are also named: Wilson's Warbler, Wilson's Storm-Petrel, and Wilson's Phalarope. Wilson, along with his notable contemporary John James Audubon, was among the principal founders of the study of ornithology in North America.

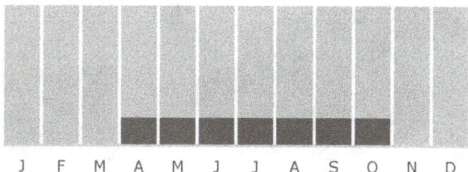

J F M A M J J A S O N D

⑤ **BLUE JAY.** *Cyanocitta cristata.*

SIZE: 11 in.

HABITAT: Any type of woods, but especially open woods and edges. Also common in all variety of wooded urban and suburban areas.

WILD DIET: Insects and spiders, nuts, grains, and seeds. May scavenge nearly anything else.

BEHAVIOR: Among the most visible of suburban birds, this species is noisy, active, and brightly colored. Jays are relatives of crows and ravens, and consequently possess many highly intelligent traits, such as intricate structuring of social systems, food caching, and accurate mimicry of other birds and animals. The raucous *jeer* of this species may carry for hundreds of yards across quiet sections of habitat.

MIGRATE? Partially.

NESTING: Selects a location amid the thick branches of a tree, about 10-20 ft. above the ground. Cup-shaped, constructed with soft twigs and grasses, and lined with plant roots. About 6-8 in. across, sometimes sprawling larger.

EGGS: Shades of blue to blue-green, with dirty mottling. Length of 1 in. Total of 3-6, sometimes with a second brood.

BIRD FEEDING TIPS

FEEDER DIET: Black-oil and hulled sunflower seeds, suet, safflower seed, mealworms, cracked corn, peanuts and peanut hearts, fruit, millet, milo. **FEEDER TYPES**: Platforms, suet cages, ground, hoppers, tubes. **FEEDER BEHAVIOR**: May yield to other birds when feeder is contested. Does not usually stay for long, unless very familiar with the surroundings.

COMPARE TO SIMILAR SPECIES: Distinct color and patterning for its size.

DID YOU KNOW? Blue Jays often push acorns into the ground during the fall months, saving them for colder days ahead. In fact, it is believed that this habit helped oak trees to recolonize much of North America following the last ice age.

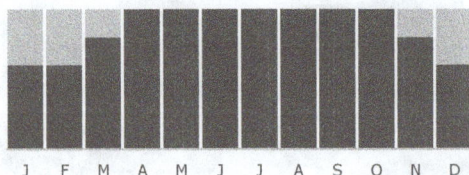

J F M A M J J A S O N D

Adults at top and bottom.

Male at top (Photo by Greg Hume / CC BY-SA / Cropped),
Female at bottom (Photo by Andrew Dimler / CC BY-SA / Cropped).

① AMERICAN KESTREL. *Falco sparverius.*

SIZE: 11 in.

HABITAT: Open fields, including rural farmland and overgrown pasture. Occasionally, cities and suburbs.

WILD DIET: Insects (e.g., grasshoppers), small rodents (e.g., voles, mice) and birds, reptiles, and amphibians.

BEHAVIOR: Often observed scanning the ground from a perch, which may be a wire, post, fence, or exposed tree branch. It quickly dives or hovers as it approaches prey, which is usually struck directly on the ground. Upon returning to a perch, the kestrel consumes its prey piecemeal while holding it securely with one talon. Over a dozen catches may be made in a single hour, depending on the size and variety of prey targeted. Fastidious birders may also notice that individual kestrels tend to perfect their own hunting habits and techniques, similar to the behavior sometimes exhibited by the Peregrine Falcon, its much larger relative.

MIGRATE? Yes.

NESTING: Nests in various cavities, which may be old woodpecker hollows, rock crevices, or nooks in corners of buildings. No nest materials are used.

EGGS: Light brown or off-white, with dirty mottling. Length of 1 ½ in. Total of 3-6, occasionally with a second brood.

FEEDER BEHAVIOR: Rarely hunts at feeders.

COMPARE TO SIMILAR SPECIES: Though the size of a Mourning Dove, this species has bright, colorful markings (especially on males, which feature a bright orange chest and upper back) and a distinctive face. These facial markings, as well as their narrow, pointed wings in flight (characteristic of falcons, such as the Peregrine), help to differentiate from the Sharp-shinned Hawk.

DID YOU KNOW? The American Kestrel is the smallest of all North American falconids, and is hunted by all manner of larger falcons, owls, and hawks, even including the diminutive Sharp-shinned Hawk on occasion.

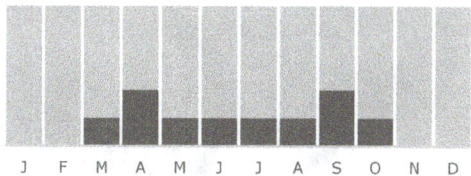

J F M A M J J A S O N D

⑤ **AMERICAN ROBIN.** *Turdus migratorius.*

SIZE: 10 in.

HABITAT: Open woods, parks, suburbs.

WILD DIET: Insects and spiders, worms, berries, and fruits.

BEHAVIOR: Often seen on suburban lawns, darting and pausing as it passes through the grass, and pulling worms from the soil. Particularly active immediately after rainfall (when worms move to the surface) or lawn mowing. Sings its undulating, cheery melodies of chirps for long periods while perched in trees. During colder months, may flock in very large groups to cooperatively search for food sources.

MIGRATE? Partially.

NESTING: Finds a location with ample leaf cover or protection, typically in trees or in artificial structures such as gutters, eaves, or streetlights. Cup-shaped, and composed of twigs and vegetation. About 6 in. across and 4 in. deep.

EGGS: Bright, light blue. Length of 1 in. Total of 3-5. Usually raises 2 broods each year, but may raise up to 3.

BIRD FEEDING TIPS

FEEDER DIET: Hulled sunflower seeds, suet, safflower seed, mealworms, fruit, peanut hearts. **FEEDER TYPES**: Ground, platforms. **FEEDER BEHAVIOR**: Very rarely visits feeders, but is frequently observable trotting through nearby lawns, gardens, and mulch beds.

COMPARE TO SIMILAR SPECIES: Juvenile could be confused with a Wood Thrush, but orange on chest and dark-colored head remain distinctive. Adults are quite distinctive and familiar.

DID YOU KNOW? The song of the American Robin has long been associated with the coming of spring, at which time males begin to vociferously seek out mates and defend their breeding territories. Emily Dickinson was especially fond of using this species as an allusion to springtime, with her poems ""Hope" is the thing with feathers" and "I dreaded that first robin so" serving as notable examples.

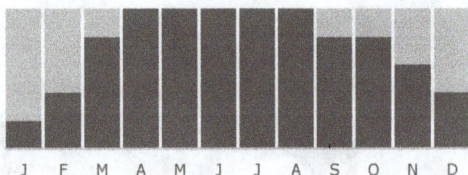

J F M A M J J A S O N D

Adult at top,
Juvenile at bottom (Photo by K6ka / CC BY-SA / Cropped).

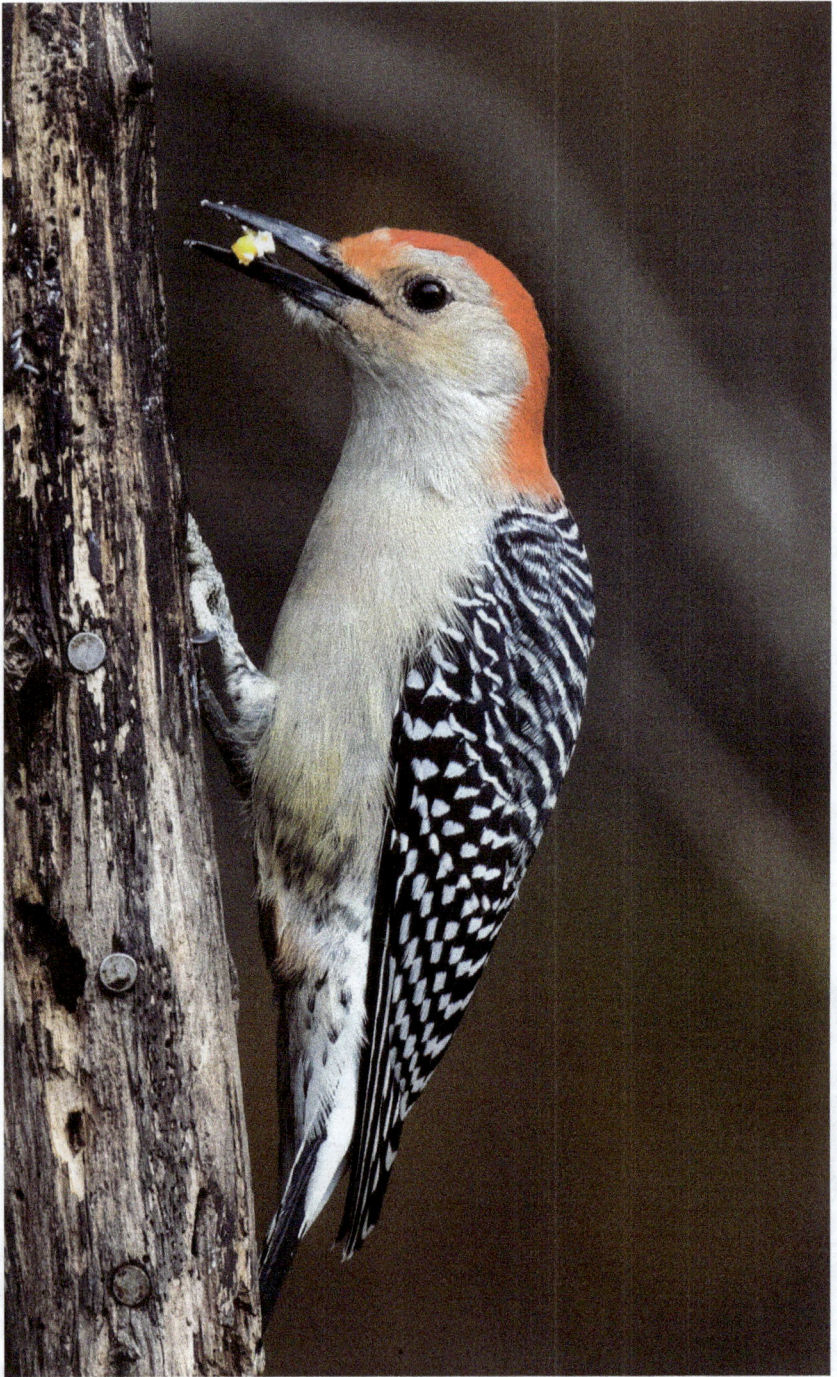

Adult male feeding (Note that females have a red patch which extends only partway
up the back of the neck, and juveniles often have gray coloration on part or all of patch).

③ # RED-BELLIED WOODPECKER.
Melanerpes carolinus.

SIZE: 9 ¾ in.

HABITAT: Various woods, wooded suburbs.

WILD DIET: Insects and spiders, seeds, nuts, fruits and berries.

BEHAVIOR: Like most woodpeckers, this species hops up and down tree trunks in search of food hidden beneath and between pieces of bark, using its sturdily built tail as a brace to facilitate such movements. Individuals are usually observed in a right-side-up position: inspecting, hammering, and then quickly grabbing food with the tongue. Individuals also frequently cache food in knots or crevices of trees.

MIGRATE? No.

NESTING: May select the trunk of a dead tree used in past years, but excavates a new nest cavity each year. Forms an entrance hole about 4 in. across, and a cavity 1 ft. deep.

EGGS: Shades of white. Length of 1 in. Total of 3-5. Usually raises 1-2 broods each year, but occasionally attempts to hatch and raise a third.

BIRD FEEDING TIPS

FEEDER DIET: Suet, black-oil and hulled sunflower seeds, peanuts and peanut hearts, safflower seed, cracked corn, grape jelly, mealworms, fruit, sugar water. **FEEDER TYPES**: Suet cages, tubes, hoppers, platforms, nectar feeders. **FEEDER BEHAVIOR**: Readily takes suet like many other woodpeckers, though may be present at other feeders as well. May assert its dominance and force other birds to scatter when it lands on a feeder.

COMPARE TO SIMILAR SPECIES: Individuals are often confused with Red-headed Woodpeckers, which possess an entirely red head and neck, rather than just a patch on top. Compared to the Northern Flicker, this species is slightly smaller and has different markings and coloration.

DID YOU KNOW? Due to its preference for building a nest cavity in dead trees, the Red-bellied Woodpecker is particularly vulnerable to the clearing of established woodlots and dying stands of forest.

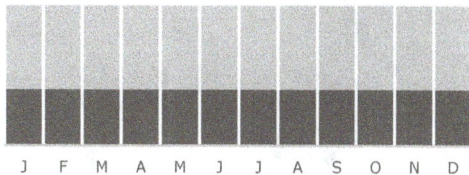

J F M A M J J A S O N D

③ **KILLDEER.** *Charadrius vociferus.*

SIZE: 9 ½ in.

HABITAT: Fields, mudflats, wetlands, and beaches.

WILD DIET: Insects (e.g., beetles, flies), small aquatic invertebrates, worms.

BEHAVIOR: A plover of the ball fields, this species is one of the few shorebirds which regularly visits the rural suburbs. Often flocks when feeding, alternatingly running and pausing as each individual intently searches for food. When taking its invertebrate prey, the Killdeer either snaps up the item with its bill or yanks it forcefully from the substrate. Lone members of the flock aerially rove about nearby, seeking as-yet undiscovered feeding sites. Scatters quickly when approached. When flying, emits its characteristic, squeaky *kill-dee-ur* call.

MIGRATE? Yes.

NESTING: A shallow rut is scraped into the ground, upon which the eggs are laid. Close to 3 in. across.

EGGS: Whitish-tan, with many large black markings. Length of 1 ½ in. Total of 4-7. May raise 1-3 broods each year, but usually raises 2.

FEEDER BEHAVIOR: Does not visit feeders.

COMPARE TO SIMILAR SPECIES: Long, straight legs help to distinguish this as a shorebird; among other shorebirds and plovers, note this species' large size and two black chest rings (compared to the Semipalmated Plover's one).

DID YOU KNOW? During the breeding season, the Killdeer is well known for diverting predators' attention away from its nests by utilizing several notable display tactics. It may use "broken-wing" displays to lure a predator away before taking evasive flight, or alternatively spread its feathers and directly charge the intruder. However, it is best to watch from a safe distance: *never* closely approach bird nests, as this can adversely affect breeding success.

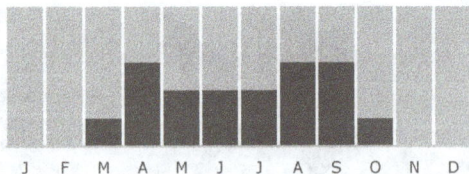

J F M A M J J A S O N D

Adult wading at top,
Adults in flight at bottom (Photo by Magnus Manske / CC BY-SA).

Male at top,
Female at bottom (Photo by Simon Wray / CC BY-SA).

④ **HAIRY WOODPECKER.** *Dryobates villosus.*

SIZE: 9 ¼ in.

HABITAT: Woods, especially dense, mature woods. Sometimes suburbs and parks.

WILD DIET: Mostly insects and larvae, but also nuts, seeds, and berries.

BEHAVIOR: Feeds by boring holes into tree bark, as well as by prying off slabs of bark with its bill. Often prefers to rest high in mature tree stands, which can make this species difficult to spot. In addition, this species' rapid-fire drilling pattern is among the fastest of all woodpeckers' (about 25 to 30 beats per minute), which can assist with identification once a few species have been compared in the field.

MIGRATE? No.

NESTING: Drills a cavity in a dead or decaying tree. Forms an entrance hole about 2 in. across, with a cavity extending about 1 ft. deep.

EGGS: Shades of white. Length of 1 in. Total of 3-5.

BIRD FEEDING TIPS

FEEDER DIET: Suet, black-oil and hulled sunflower seeds, peanuts and peanut hearts, mealworms, safflower seed. **FEEDER TYPES**: Suet cages, tubes, hoppers, platforms. **FEEDER BEHAVIOR**: May take time to attract, but will often return after first visiting. Mostly eats suet. Can also engage in mild acrobatics on feeders when reaching for seed.

COMPARE TO SIMILAR SPECIES: Nearly identical to Downy Woodpecker, apart from its notably larger average size. Other key differences include a bill which is about as long as the length of its head (rather than smaller), and possession of clean outer white tail feathers (rather than spotted).

DID YOU KNOW? This species may be attracted by the dozens to sections of forest experiencing mass beetle infestations. Though not often witnessed, this spectacle is a wonderful opportunity to observe the Hairy for extended periods.

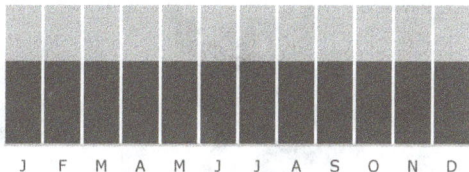

J F M A M J J A S O N D

① **EASTERN MEADOWLARK.** *Sturnella magna.*

SIZE: 9 in.

HABITAT: Overgrown fields, grasslands, and prairies.

WILD DIET: Mostly insects, but also seeds and grains (particularly in the winter).

BEHAVIOR: Best known for whistling its distinctive song from elevated perches during breeding season, but is usually less noticeable throughout the remainder of the year, especially in the North. While walking across the ground, forages by probing and prying apart the soil in search of a variety of insects; it accomplishes this feat with its considerably strong jaw muscles. Polygynous by nature, each male will defend a territory of two to three resident females, each with whom he will mate.

MIGRATE? Yes.

NESTING: Selects a small rut in the ground, and constructs nest on top. Cup-shaped, with stems and grasses used. About 8 in. across and 2 in. deep.

EGGS: White to light blue, with brown mottling. Length of 1 in. Total of 3-6, with 2 broods.

BIRD FEEDING TIPS

FEEDER DIET: Cracked corn, hulled sunflower seeds. **FEEDER TYPES:** Ground. **FEEDER BEHAVIOR:** Very uncommon at feeders. Visits are typically during wintertime, when insects are scarce.

COMPARE TO SIMILAR SPECIES: The Western Meadowlark is nearly identical to the Eastern, though their ranges only overlap in the western Midwest U.S. These species are best differentiated by song (Western has flute-like, more garbled two-phrase song, compared to Eastern's higher, clear, one-phrase whistles), though the former is also unreliably identified by the brown lines across its head, which are lighter. Also, this species is somewhat similar to the Dickcissel, but larger size, fully yellow belly, and longer bill are distinct to the meadowlarks.

DID YOU KNOW? While Western Meadowlarks sing about a dozen variations of their common melody, Easterns can have repertoires of over 100 different, but consistent, patterns—each of which still resembles the original song.

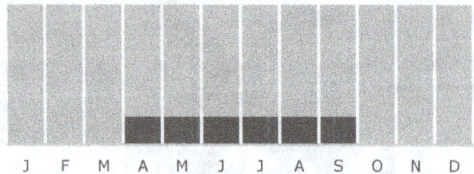

J F M A M J J A S O N D

Adults at top and bottom.

Adult male at top (Photo by D. Faulder / CC BY-SA / Cropped),
Adult female at bottom (Photo by David A. Mitchell / CC BY-SA).

① **PINE GROSBEAK.** *Pinicola enucleator.*

SIZE: 9 in.

HABITAT: Open coniferous woods. During winter irruptions (*See* Migrate), may also visit mixed woods and suburbs.

WILD DIET: Fruits, seeds, buds. Rarely, insects.

BEHAVIOR: This species often hops or walks along branches or the ground, foraging for fruits and seeds; its seeming lack of volition has led some eastern Canadians to nickname this bird the "mope." Primarily frugivorous, or fruit-eating, flocks (also known as grosses) may remain in a single tree until all available food has been gleaned from the branches. May consume snow to quench thirst, a habit well suited to the harsher winter months.

MIGRATE? Not usually. In the winter, may irrupt southward from central Canada in greater numbers when annual wild seed crops are lower than usual.

NESTING: Selects a location adjacent to the trunk in the branches of a conifer. Finely woven bowl of twigs and grasses. About 8 in. across.

EGGS: Light blue, with variable dark speckling. Length of 1 in. Total of 3-4.

BIRD FEEDING TIPS

FEEDER DIET: Fruit, black-oil and hulled sunflower seeds, suet. **FEEDER TYPES**: Platforms, hoppers, tubes, suet cages. **FEEDER BEHAVIOR**: Presence varies year to year, in line with food availability (*See* Migrate section). Fairly peaceable with other birds.

COMPARE TO SIMILAR SPECIES: Chunky, sharp bill and stout silhouette are very similar to its finch relatives, but its size is far larger than that of the Purple or House Finch, or the crossbills. Nearly the size of an American Robin.

DID YOU KNOW? This species was memorably featured on the back of the Canadian $1,000 bill in the late 1980s. In the illustration, a male and female are depicted on a lone branch, overlooking the scenic boreal countryside.

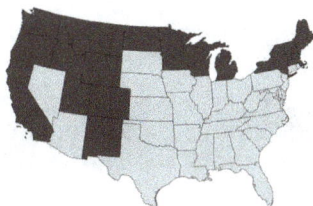

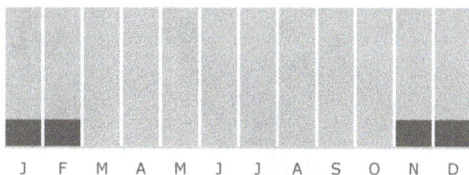

J F M A M J J A S O N D

⑤ **NORTHERN CARDINAL.** *Cardinalis cardinalis.*

SIZE: 8 ¾ in.

HABITAT: Open woods, cities and suburbs. Also, thickets and scrub.

WILD DIET: Seeds, fruits, and grains. Sometimes, insects.

BEHAVIOR: Conceivably the most photographed bird in North America, this species is often found perched in various shrubs, trees, and even in sheltered surroundings on the ground. Individuals typically stay at each foraging location for several minutes or longer. In late spring and summer, frequently sings from prominent, elevated perches to defend territory. Song is an ascending and whistled *wheet, wheet, ..., wheet*, followed immediately by a quick series of *chew, chew, ..., chew*. Also calls repeatedly with loud metallic chinks.

MIGRATE? No.

NESTING: Prefers locations with dense leaf cover, usually in a tree or shrub. Nest bowl is woven of twigs, and lined with finer grasses, stems. About 3-4 in. across.

EGGS: Off-white to light blue-green, with brown speckling or mottling. Length of 1 in. Total of 2-4, with 2-3 broods.

BIRD FEEDING TIPS

FEEDER DIET: Black-oil and hulled sunflower seeds, safflower seed, peanut hearts, cracked corn, millet, milo, suet. **FEEDER TYPES**: Platforms, hoppers, tubes, ground. **FEEDER BEHAVIOR**: Very common visitor, and one of the first species to repeatedly visit new feeders. Often observed in male-female pairs, especially during spring and summer.

COMPARE TO SIMILAR SPECIES: Male Summer and Scarlet Tanagers are also bright red—particularly the former—but the Northern Cardinal is larger, has a black mask, and has a conspicuous head crest.

DID YOU KNOW? In May and June, cardinals are very territorial toward other individuals of the same species, periodically going so far as to attack their own reflections in windows or panes of glass. Other species—particularly those which nest in the suburbs, such as the American Robin—have also been known to occasionally engage in similar behaviors.

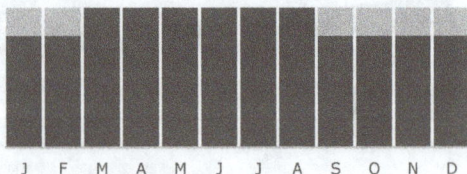

J F M A M J J A S O N D

Adult male at top,
Adult female at bottom left,
Juvenile female at bottom right.

Adults at top and bottom.

④ **GRAY CATBIRD.** *Dumetella carolinensis.*

SIZE: 8 ¾ in.

HABITAT: Thickets, edges of woods, overgrown fields, and suburbs.

WILD DIET: Fruits and berries (e.g., holly berries, poison ivy), and insects.

BEHAVIOR: This species is ordinarily sequestered away in tangles of shrubs and vines, hopping about while gleaning fruits and berries from the branches or ground. Most easily recognizable due to its repeated, raspy mewing call—rather like that of a cantankerous feline.

MIGRATE? Yes.

NESTING: Concealed in dense shrub foliage. Bowl of twigs and dried grasses, and lined with softer materials, such as pine needles. About 5-6 in. across.

EGGS: Bright turquoise. Length of 1 in. Total of 1-5, with 2 broods.

BIRD FEEDING TIPS

FEEDER DIET: Mealworms, suet, grape jelly, fruit. **FEEDER TYPES**: Ground, platforms, suet cages. **FEEDER BEHAVIOR**: Uncommon visitor, but known to retrieve suet droppings from ground. Particularly in May and June, may also take mealworms and fruit from platforms.

COMPARE TO SIMILAR SPECIES: Most similar to the larger Northern Mockingbird, but note the Gray Catbird's distinct black head cap, lack of white barring on wings, and overall darker silhouette.

DID YOU KNOW? It is thought that most catbirds which nest along the Atlantic Seaboard winter in Florida or the Caribbean, and that most Midwestern birds migrate to wintering grounds in Central America. Once the winter is complete, the flocks return to the same local territories where they spent the previous summer—possibly even visiting the same backyards year after year.

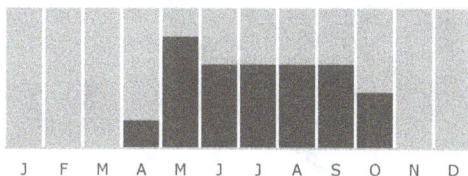

J F M A M J J A S O N D

② EASTERN KINGBIRD. *Tyrannus tyrannus.*

SIZE: 8 ¼ in.

HABITAT: Fields, edges of woods; often adjacent to lakes, rivers, and wetlands.

WILD DIET: Insects (e.g., dragonflies, crickets). Very occasionally, small fruits.

BEHAVIOR: This species is usually spotted in semi-open country near a water source, perched on the branch of a tree or large bush. It periodically sallies out for insect prey, which is taken both aerially and from swoops near the ground. Individuals usually return to the same perch, even after departures lasting as long as a minute, unless insects are sparse—in which case, a new perch is instead located. Commonly sings with clipped, sputtering notes punctuated by ascending *dzee* notes. Known to flock in groups of several dozen, occasionally larger, during migration periods. As its Latin name suggests, this species is a veritable tyrant in the course of defending its breeding territory from predators and even other kingbirds.

MIGRATE? Yes.

NESTING: Trees and shrubs, at varying heights. Woven cup of dried grasses and twigs, and lined with softer vegetative materials. About 5-6 in. across.

EGGS: Off-white, with large red-brown splotches, usually clustered on oblong side. Length of 1 in. Total of 2-5.

FEEDER BEHAVIOR: Does not visit feeders.

COMPARE TO SIMILAR SPECIES: Much larger than the similarly colored Eastern Phoebe, as well as most other flycatchers.

DID YOU KNOW? The Eastern Kingbird winters in Central and South America, where it breaks with established routine and feeds on an array of small fruits and berries. These wintering sites are mostly concentrated in the western Amazon, and coincide with the wet season—with some localities receiving upwards of 100 inches of rain in just a few months. Fruits quickly begin to burst from their buds all throughout the rainforest—just in time for the famished, travel-wearied kingbird.

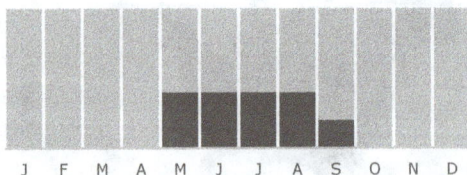

J F M A M J J A S O N D

Adults at top and bottom.

Breeding adult at top (Jan. to Aug.),
Nonbreeding adult at bottom left (Sept. to Jan.),
Flock at bottom right (Photo by John Holmes / CC BY-SA / Cropped).

④ EUROPEAN STARLING. *Sturnus vulgaris.*

SIZE: 8 ¼ in.

HABITAT: Cities and suburbs, agricultural fields. Often perched on power lines.

WILD DIET: Mostly insects (e.g., grasshoppers, flies) and spiders. Also, fruit and berries, seeds, grains, and garbage.

BEHAVIOR: This invasive species from Europe is most commonly observed in large, wheeling flocks of hundreds, or even thousands, which swarm across the sky—a flocking motion once described by the poet Dante Alighieri as seemingly being pushed by gusts of wind. These birds may forage in agricultural fields, on recently mowed lawns, or in urban centers, exhausting local resources before moving on. Calls include harsh chattering, buzzing, whistling, and rattling noises.

MIGRATE? No.

NESTING: Cavity nester. Selected cavities may include manmade openings (e.g., streetlights), former woodpecker nests, and nest boxes. A shallow bowl is formed inside, constructed of dried grasses. On average, about 8 in. wide.

EGGS: Light blue-green. Length of 1 in. Total of 4-6, with 2 broods.

BIRD FEEDING TIPS

FEEDER DIET: Black-oil and hulled sunflower seeds, suet, cracked corn, peanuts and peanut hearts, millet, oats, milo, fruit. **FEEDER TYPES**: Platforms, hoppers, tubes, ground, suet cages. **FEEDER BEHAVIOR**: Can quickly overrun feeders, a circumstance which can be averted by solely offering safflower seed at some stations. Also, may use nest boxes.

COMPARE TO SIMILAR SPECIES: Very distinctive appearance and profile, particularly when forming large flocks, and rather unlike most other regional species.

DID YOU KNOW? About 100 starlings were originally introduced to Central Park in 1890 and 1891 by Shakespeare enthusiasts, in homage to a brief account of the species in *Henry IV*. In the years since, however, they have established themselves as one of the most abundant species continent-wide, which has led to the concomitant decline of many native cavity-nesting species, such as the Purple Martin.

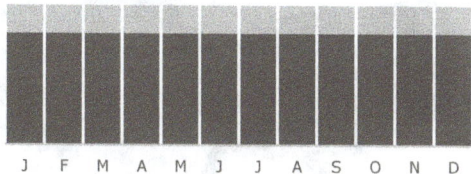

J F M A M J J A S O N D

⑤ RED-WINGED BLACKBIRD.

Agelaius phoeniceus.

SIZE: 8 in.

HABITAT: Marshes and ponds, flooded fields, weedy fields. Sometimes along the median strip or the roadsides of highways.

WILD DIET: Seeds and grains. In warmer months, half of diet also consists of insects.

BEHAVIOR: The archetypal wetland passerine, or perching bird, this species is known for inhabiting nearby tangles of dense brush and thicket. Opportunistically forages for insects whenever available, and otherwise is a prodigious consumer of seeds and grains. One of the most population-dense species in North America, due to the male's tendency to mate with five to 15 females, and its highly aggressive territoriality: with males known to indignantly pursue and repeatedly attack much larger birds, such as crows and hawks. Song is a *kok-a-reeee*, with particular emphasis and length placed on the final, slurred and trilled syllable. This rattling din is just about inescapable in wetter environs.

MIGRATE? Mostly.

NESTING: Weaves a neat cup of grasses and reeds, often amid tall shoots of vegetation. About 6 in. across and 4 in. deep.

EGGS: Light turquoise, with dark markings. Length of 1 in. Total of 2-4. Raises 1-3 broods each year, usually 2.

BIRD FEEDING TIPS

FEEDER DIET: Black-oil and hulled sunflower seeds, cracked corn, suet, peanut hearts, oats, millet, milo. **FEEDER TYPES**: Suet cages, platforms, hoppers, tubes. **FEEDER BEHAVIOR**: Most likely to visit in late fall to mid-spring, when insects are less plentiful.

COMPARE TO SIMILAR SPECIES: Male's red-orange wing patch is highly distinctive; female is much smaller and more sparrow-like, but notice her sharp, pointed bill, as well as the defined, light eyeline.

DID YOU KNOW? Males with larger red wing patches are more aggressive and better at defending their territories from rivals. This likely serves as a biological signaling mechanism, and is produced by dietary carotenoid pigments; in fact, this same class of pigments gives carrots their familiar orange hue.

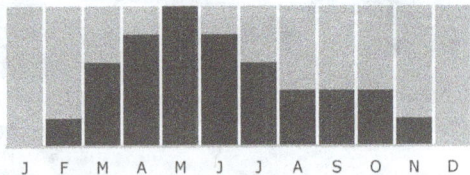

J F M A M J J A S O N D

Adult male at top,
Adult female at bottom left,
Juvenile male at bottom right (Notice "in-between," dirty stage of coloration).

Adult male performing a scratch-and-hop at top,
Adult female at bottom (Photo by Shawn Taylor / CC BY-SA / Cropped).

① EASTERN TOWHEE. *Pipilo erythrophthalmus.*

SIZE: 8 in.

HABITAT: Mostly thickets—in open woods, overgrown fields, and hedgerows.

WILD DIET: Seeds, fruits, buds, insects and spiders, and snails.

BEHAVIOR: This oversized sparrow moves slowly, but noisily, through understories of woods and overgrown fields. Over three-quarters of foraging is conducted on the ground, with occasional forays onto low branches. Prefers to strip away leaf litter to uncover potential food items, often using a characteristic two-legged, backward scratch-and-hop motion. Given the dense cover of its typical habitat, this species is more often seen than heard. Its song resembles *drink-your-teeeeaaaa*, with the final syllable high and trilled; the call is a squeaky, yanking, and ascending *chewink*.

MIGRATE? Yes.

NESTING: Selects a concealed location on the ground, with the nest sunken into leaf litter amid surrounding vegetation. Finely woven bowl of twigs, grasses, and stems. About 4-5 in. across.

EGGS: Off-white or light pink, with dense, light brown spotting. Length of 1 in. Total of 2-6. Raises 1-3 broods each year, usually 2.

BIRD FEEDING TIPS

FEEDER DIET: Black-oil and hulled sunflower seeds, cracked corn, peanut hearts, millet, milo, suet. **FEEDER TYPES**: Ground, platforms. **FEEDER BEHAVIOR**: Most common in yards with dense shrubbery or hedgerows, particularly near woods with a thicketed understory. Animatedly scratches along the ground for seeds.

COMPARE TO SIMILAR SPECIES: Spotted Towhee of the Great Plains is similar, but has extensive white spotting along the wing. In addition, American Robin also has orange on underside, but Eastern Towhee has a bright white belly.

DID YOU KNOW? The towhee's common name is onomatopoeic, specifically relating to its *towhee* call, which is more often described as a *chewink* (*See* Behavior).

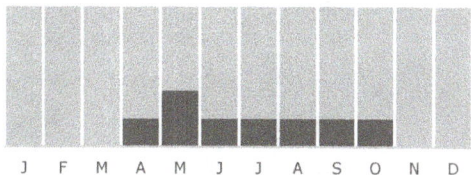

J F M A M J J A S O N D

③ ROSE-BREASTED GROSBEAK.

Pheucticus ludovicianus.

SIZE: 8 in.

HABITAT: Mostly dense or thicketed woods, also tree-dense parks. During migration, common in suburbs and open woods as well.

WILD DIET: Insects (e.g., beetles, ants), berries (e.g., blackberries, mulberries), seeds, buds, and grains.

BEHAVIOR: Often found in the treetops or amid dense foliage, carefully gleaning any suitable insects or vegetative matter as it hops along. Sings a swooping, up-and-down melody reminiscent of that of the American Robin, but seemingly with more flourishes.

MIGRATE? Yes.

NESTING: Selects a location in the vertical fork of tree branches. Messy cup, woven with twigs. About 7-8 in. across.

EGGS: Off-white to light blue-green, with red-brown spotting. Length of 1 in. Total of 3-4, sometimes with a second brood.

BIRD FEEDING TIPS

FEEDER DIET: Black-oil and hulled sunflower seeds, safflower seed, peanut hearts, cracked corn, oats, millet, milo. **FEEDER TYPES**: Platforms, hoppers, tubes, ground. **FEEDER BEHAVIOR**: Most conspicuous in spring migration, during which large groups are making their way north, and tend to be less fussy regarding habitat selection. Behaves similarly to cardinals, with usual visits of up to a minute and a generally wary disposition.

COMPARE TO SIMILAR SPECIES: Male is highly distinctive. Female may superficially resemble some finches, sparrows, or cowbirds, but has a far stouter bill, pronounced white eyebrow line, and delicate streaking across a pale chest.

DID YOU KNOW? Unlike most birds, the male shares nest incubation responsibilities with the female—often singing happily while doing so.

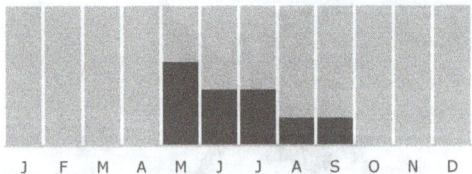

J F M A M J J A S O N D

Adult male at top (Photo by Johnathan Nightingale / CC BY-SA / Cropped),
Adult female at bottom (Photo by Shawn Taylor / CC BY-SA / Cropped).

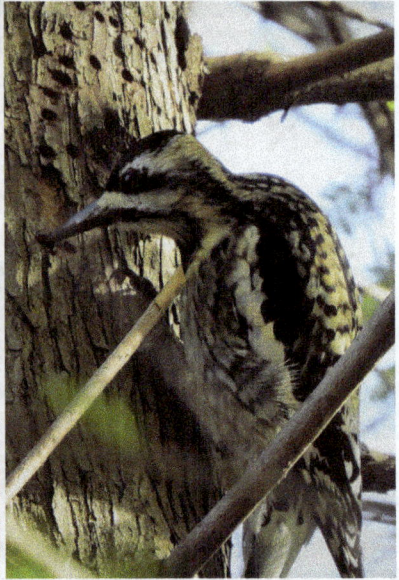

Adult female at top (Notice white throat),
Adult male at bottom left (Notice red throat),
Juvenile at bottom right.

② YELLOW-BELLIED SAPSUCKER.

Sphyrapicus varius.

SIZE: 8 in.

HABITAT: Dense to semi-open woods. Often favors woods with plenty of younger, faster-growing trees. Sometimes, orchards.

WILD DIET: Sap, insects (e.g., carpenter ants) and spiders. Sometimes, fruit.

BEHAVIOR: This species drills neat rows of shallow, narrow wells into the inner tissue of tree trunks. These wells are constantly maintained to keep the sap flowing, and further rows are drilled in productive trees to form ordered, dotlike grids. Trees which are frequently used include maples, birches, hickories, and poplars. May also feed on flying insects, and any ants attracted to their sap wells. Idiosyncratic drumming pattern is erratic, and sounds rather like the transmission of an esoteric Morse code message.

MIGRATE? Yes.

NESTING: Excavates a cavity in a dying or decaying tree. Entrance is less than 2 in. across, and nest hole is approximately 9 in. deep.

EGGS: White. Length of 1 in. Total of 4-7.

BIRD FEEDING TIPS

FEEDER DIET: Grape jelly, suet, sugar water, mealworms. **FEEDER TYPES**: Suet cages, platforms, nectar feeders. **FEEDER BEHAVIOR**: Uncommon visitor, but may be regularly attracted by small cups of grape jelly or sugar water, as well as by suet cages.

COMPARE TO SIMILAR SPECIES: Head patterning is particularly distinctive.

DID YOU KNOW? Other species actively benefit from the prolific drilling of sapsuckers, including the porcupines, squirrels, nuthatches, and bats which readily take advantage of the accompanying gratis food source. In addition, hummingbirds have even been known to time spring migrations in line with those of sapsuckers, with breeding success increased by the local presence of open sap wells.

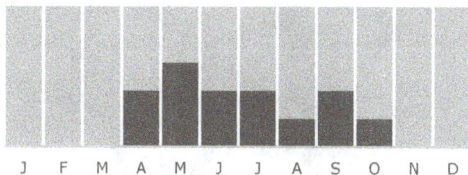

J F M A M J J A S O N D

② **WOOD THRUSH.** *Hylocichla mustelina.*

SIZE: 7 ¾ in.

HABITAT: Mature, dense woods. Less commonly, open woods and parks.

WILD DIET: Insects (e.g., beetles, caterpillars, ants), fruit (e.g., elderberries), snails.

BEHAVIOR: This thrush is usually found foraging by itself, sorting through leaf litter with its bill or clambering over low shrubs in search of berries. Individuals are often wary of potential threats, and quickly hop along the forest floor. The Wood Thrush is perhaps best known for its empyrean, bitonal *ee-o-lay* song, which sounds as if it is produced by a duet of skillful flutists. Males usually sing from exposed perches, allowing the melody to drift for acres.

MIGRATE? Yes.

NESTING: Selects a densely vegetated location hidden among the branches of a shrub or low tree. A bowl is woven of twigs and fine grasses, and bound together on the interior with some mud. About 5-6 in. across.

EGGS: Bright turquoise. Length of 1 in. Total of 3-4, with 1-2 broods.

FEEDER BEHAVIOR: Does not visit feeders.

COMPARE TO SIMILAR SPECIES: Similar to other medium-sized thrushes, including the juvenile American Robin, the Veery, the Swainson's Thrush, and the Hermit Thrush. The Wood Thrush is best identified by its red-brown upper side, its white belly with dark, well-defined brown spots, and its brownish, patterned cheek.

DID YOU KNOW? This species has declined significantly over the past number of decades. Nest failures due to the encroachment of Brown-headed Cowbirds is a result of increasing woodland fragmentation, which decreases the amount of deep forest habitat suitable for nesting. Additionally, an academic study coauthored by Miyoko Chu and Stefan Hames of the Cornell Lab of Ornithology has suggested that acid rain may be a supplementary factor, with fewer land snails now available as a calcium source for thrushes when egg-laying.

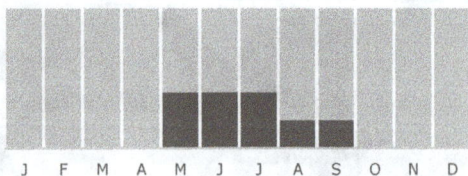

J F M A M J J A S O N D

Adult at top and bottom.

Adult male at top,
Adult female at bottom (Note: Juveniles are slightly drabber, buffier by comparison).

③ **BALTIMORE ORIOLE.** *Icterus galbula.*

SIZE: 7 ¾ in.

HABITAT: Open woods, suburbs, parks, and orchards.

WILD DIET: Berries and fruits, insects, and nectar.

BEHAVIOR: Best known for its penchant for gleaning berries and fruits from trees and bushes all across its territory, this species actually takes more insects than fruits during the breeding season—in keeping with the young's higher protein needs. Busily clambers and clings from all angles as it forages for such items as caterpillars, mulberries, and grapes. When feeding on larger fruits, it punctures the surface with its bill, before opening and slurping with deft strokes of its brushlike tongue. In springtime, particularly well-known for its chattering, flute-like whistles.

MIGRATE? Yes.

NESTING: In the upper reaches of a tree, weaves a hanging, bindle-like nest of fine grasses and hairs: a marvel of construction. About 4 in. across and 5 in. deep.

EGGS: Off-white to blue-green, with dark streaking and splotches. Length of 1 in. Total of 3-6.

BIRD FEEDING TIPS

FEEDER DIET: Fruit, grape jelly, sugar water, suet. **FEEDER TYPES:** Platforms, nectar feeders. **FEEDER BEHAVIOR:** Prefers to take orange slices and grape jelly from small platform cups. Also visits nectar feeders. Ceteris paribus, usually attracted to the color orange. More likely to visit feeders outside of breeding season.

COMPARE TO SIMILAR SPECIES: Among males, bright orange underside (compared to smaller Orchard Oriole's dark orange) and full black head and neck are diagnostic. Females have washed-out, yellow-orange coloration on the chest and belly—the only oriole dames with a fully orange-hued underside—and a dirty head and back.

DID YOU KNOW? Despite its fiery plumage, this species is actually a member of the blackbird, or icterid, family.

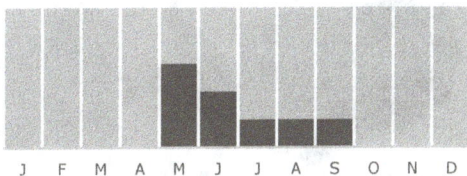

J F M A M J J A S O N D

③ BROWN-HEADED COWBIRD. *Molothrus ater.*

SIZE: 7 ½ in.

HABITAT: Edges of woods, open fields, suburbs.

WILD DIET: Seeds, grains, insects. Sometimes eggs of other birds.

BEHAVIOR: Often announces its presence with a short, liquid-like chortle, immediately followed by a thin, high whistle. Customarily forages on the ground, and may also be found perching in trees and bushes. In fields, known to snap up insects disturbed by grazing livestock. Males and females both practice promiscuous mating, with few seasonally established pairs. Juveniles hatch sooner than the young of their host nests (*See* Nesting), and mature much more rapidly; this allows the young cowbird to monopolize resources and frequently outcompete the other members of its cohort.

MIGRATE? Yes.

NESTING: Brood parasite: lays eggs in nests of other birds, usually smaller species (e.g., sparrows, warblers).

EGGS: Off-white, with dense brown speckling. Length of 1 in. Total of 1-4 per nest, with up to 40 eggs per season.

BIRD FEEDING TIPS

FEEDER DIET: Black-oil and hulled sunflower seeds, cracked corn, peanut hearts, suet, millet, oats, milo. **FEEDER TYPES:** Ground, platforms, hoppers, tubes, suet cages. **FEEDER BEHAVIOR:** A highly opportunistic forager, this species is a partisan of feeder setups of nearly all varieties, and may also congregate on the ground for spilled feed. From May to July, juveniles are often observed following adoptive mothers of other species.

COMPARE TO SIMILAR SPECIES: Notice male's distinctive brown head and neck; females and juveniles are duller brown and sparrow-like, but are drabber and lack extensive, well-defined streaking. Also, notice this species' characteristically stout bill, another useful field mark.

DID YOU KNOW? It is thought that the Brown-headed Cowbird's parasitic nesting behavior originally evolved due to necessity, having previously subsisted by following grazing bison across the Great Plains. As it was never in one location for more than a few weeks, it was thus not able to incubate its own young—relying on other species for this task. However, with the fragmentation of woodland due to human development (and the consequent creation of new fringe habitat), this species' further proliferation has seriously threatened populations of many woodland songbirds.

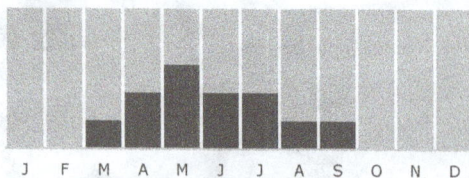

J F M A M J J A S O N D

Adult male at top,
Adult female at bottom,
Juveniles taking food from adoptive Common Yellowthroat mother, inset.

Breeding adult at top,
Chick climbing over a stone at bottom left,
Nonbreeding adult at bottom right.

② SPOTTED SANDPIPER. *Actitis macularius.*

SIZE: 7 ½ in.

HABITAT: Edges of rivers, ponds, and streams. Also, coastlines of oceans, lakes, and reservoirs. Seems to prefer rockier shorelines.

WILD DIET: Mostly insects and insect larvae. Also, small aquatic invertebrates.

BEHAVIOR: Steadily bobs its rear half as it goes about its day, a highly manifest and diagnostic behavior for this species. Often walks in seemingly undeliberate paths near the edge of the water or over rocks—until a quick pecking motion toward prey betrays the earnestness of its original intention. May take insects from the water surface, or even from midair. Usually found by itself or in small groups, though it is likely the most common North American sandpiper, particularly inland.

MIGRATE? Yes.

NESTING: In the vicinity of the water's edge, often tucked away beneath shrubs. May be situated near Common Tern colonies in some locations. A bowl-like scrape is made in the dirt, and lined with leaves and grasses. About 4 in. across.

EGGS: Off-white with brown mottling. Length of 1 - 1 ½ in. Total of 4, sometimes with a second brood.

FEEDER BEHAVIOR: Does not visit feeders.

COMPARE TO SIMILAR SPECIES: Polka-dot pattern on chest during breeding season is very distinctive among shorebirds. In nonbreeding plumage, look for its plain brown back and sides, as well as a white belly and the accompanying white coloration which rises along the sides of its breast.

DID YOU KNOW? Spotted Sandpipers are often polyandrous breeders. In this pattern, females take several mates, laying nests for each individual male to rear. Sequential polyandry of this nature is a rare breeding practice, and limited to just a few shorebird species, of which the Spotted Sandpiper is by far the most common.

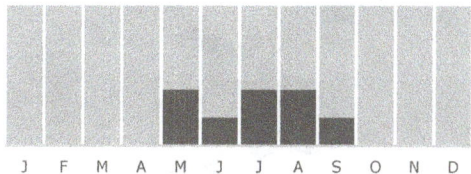

J F M A M J J A S O N D

① GREAT CRESTED FLYCATCHER.
Myiarchus crinitus.

SIZE: 7 ½ in.

HABITAT: Mature, open to semi-open woods; forest clearings.

WILD DIET: Insects (e.g., butterflies, wasps, crickets). Occasionally, small fruits.

BEHAVIOR: Perches and flies high amid the treetops, exploiting a relatively unique ecological niche among the flycatchers. Individuals sally out for insect prey for longer periods of time, and are resultantly much less likely than other flycatchers to return to the same perch. Like many flycatchers, can be entertaining to watch in flight, as it darts and swoops in close pursuit of its prey. Sometimes observed nodding its head while perched, and singing with a variety of buzzing, ascending, *breep*-like whistles.

MIGRATE? Yes.

NESTING: Cavity nester. May use natural tree hollows, former woodpecker nests, and nesting boxes. Prefers hole with a depth of 5-8 in. Inside, constructs a loosely hewn bowl of grasses, twigs, and various debris. Bowl is about 3 in. across.

EGGS: Off-white to pink, with extensive dark red-brown splotching. Length of ¾ in. Total of 4-7.

FEEDER BEHAVIOR: Does not visit feeders, but does use nest boxes.

COMPARE TO SIMILAR SPECIES: Yellow belly, conspicuous crest, and rufous tail distinguish from other flycatchers.

DID YOU KNOW? This species is known to weave molted snakeskins into its nests whenever possible, particularly in regions where there are more prolific snake populations, such as in Georgia, Louisiana, and Florida. Some titmice also practice this behavior, which may attempt to discourage ovivorous (or egg-eating) trespassers from frequenting the nest.

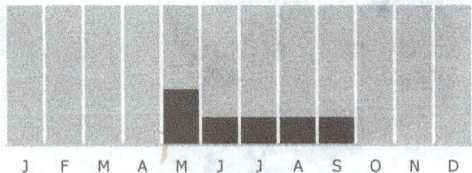

J F M A M J J A S O N D

Adults at top and bottom.

Female and male at top (Photo by Martyne Reesman / CC BY-SA / Cropped),
Male eating black-oil sunflower seeds at bottom (Photo by Paul Hurtado / CC BY-SA / Cropped).

① EVENING GROSBEAK. *Pheucticus ludovicianus.*

SIZE: 7 ½ in.

HABITAT: Mostly dense, coniferous woods. Sometimes, mixed woods and suburbs.

WILD DIET: Seeds (e.g., pine and spruce cones), insects (e.g., caterpillars, aphids), fruits and berries.

BEHAVIOR: Often found perched high in the treetops, picking apart seed cones or snapping up insects. May sometimes visit the ground or lower bushes, particularly if gleaning berries or fallen seeds. Large, sturdy bill allows for the efficient cracking of seeds that are too large for smaller species of finches.

MIGRATE? Partially, but not every year. Most stay in their territories year-round, but individuals may wander south during the winter if the annual crop of evergreen cones is insufficient. Found year-round in the northern half of Vermont, and otherwise may be observed irregularly throughout the colder months.

NESTING: Nests in forks of tree branches. Messy platform anchored to branches, which supports a tidier nest bowl. Constructed with twigs. About 6 in. across.

EGGS: Light blue-green with dirty speckling. Length of 1 in. Total of 2-5, occasionally with a second brood.

BIRD FEEDING TIPS

FEEDER DIET: Black-oil and hulled sunflower seeds. **FEEDER TYPES**: Platforms, hoppers, tubes. **FEEDER BEHAVIOR**: Much larger than most other visitors, and may command a presence when accompanied by smaller finches. Only in some years will large numbers wander south into the eastern U.S. and the far south of Canada (*See* Migrate section).

COMPARE TO SIMILAR SPECIES: The yellow and black plumage may suggest an American Goldfinch, but the Evening Grosbeak is nearly twice the size. Also, note the distinctively massive, chunky bill.

DID YOU KNOW? An Evening Grosbeak can hold a cherry with its bill while nimbly rotating and scraping away the flesh with its tongue, before cracking apart and swallowing the inner pit.

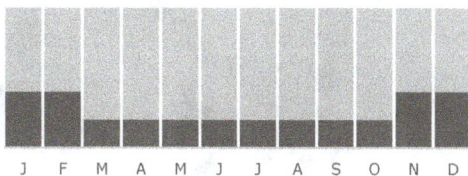

J F M A M J J A S O N D

② EASTERN BLUEBIRD. *Sialia sialis.*

SIZE: 7 ¼ in.

HABITAT: Open country with some trees, including the following settings: rural fields, parks, golf courses, roadsides, orchards, open woods, and some suburbs.

WILD DIET: Insects (e.g., grasshoppers, crickets), fruit and berries.

BEHAVIOR: Bluebirds are often found on lone or exposed perches (e.g., power lines, sign posts, tree branches), scanning the ground for insects. Once a movement has been recognized, the individual swoops to the ground, quickly takes the insect, and returns to a perch. Bluebirds may also glean fruits and berries in fall and winter, when insects are far less plentiful. A mildly varied repertoire of songs and calls includes sweet, warbling whistles and quick, raspy chattering.

MIGRATE? Partially.

NESTING: Cavity nester. Uses natural tree hollows, former woodpecker nests, and nest boxes. A plain, cramped bowl of dried grasses is woven and pressed together. Cavity is about 4-6 in. wide, with an entrance under 2 in. in diameter.

EGGS: Light blue-green. Length of ¾ in. Total of 3-7. Usually raises 2 broods each year, sometimes attempting to hatch and raise a third.

BIRD FEEDING TIPS

FEEDER DIET: Mealworms, fruit, suet, peanut hearts, black-oil and hulled sunflower seeds.
FEEDER TYPES: Platforms, tubes, ground. **FEEDER BEHAVIOR:** May gather in small flocks, particularly if live mealworms are offered. Visits yards with native berry bushes in colder months. Also, uses manmade nest boxes (*See* Nesting).

COMPARE TO SIMILAR SPECIES: Somewhat similar to the Mountain Bluebird of the Rockies, but Eastern is the only resident bluebird with an orange wash on its breast. The smaller Tufted Titmouse has a conspicuous head crest, and a greyish back and tail.

DID YOU KNOW? The Eastern Bluebird's vision is well suited to its perch-and-pursuit hunting strategy, with individuals able to spot insects from over 25 yards.

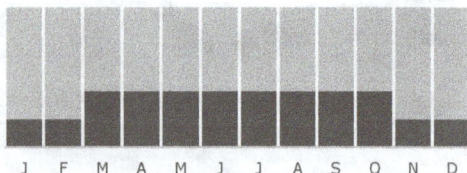

J F M A M J J A S O N D

Male at top,
Female at bottom left,
Juvenile at bottom right.

Adults at top and bottom left,
Silhouette in flight at bottom right.

③ **BARN SWALLOW.** *Hirundo rustica.*

SIZE: 7 in.

HABITAT: Various open fields (both suburban and rural), and over wetlands and lakes.

WILD DIET: Flying insects (e.g., flies, butterflies, aphids).

BEHAVIOR: Flies somewhat low over open country or water, snapping up large flying insects with its cavernous mouth. Wingbeats are quick, agile, and moderately shallow. Flocks are known to follow large machinery or livestock to feed on the insects disturbed by the activity. When flying over water, frequently dips to the surface, drinking and bathing while on the wing. Cheerfully jabbers while flying, often making *cheep* or *chureep* calls.

MIGRATE? Yes.

NESTING: Previously nested in caves, but now nests almost exclusively in barns and similar, artificial structures. Nest is composed of a mud-and-grass mixture; this dries into a relatively firm cup, which is affixed to a vertical wall or horizontal beam. May be reused in future years. About 5-8 in. across.

EGGS: Off-white or light pink, with dark brown spotting. Length of ¾ in. Total of 3-6, with 1-2 broods.

FEEDER BEHAVIOR: Does not visit feeders.

COMPARE TO SIMILAR SPECIES: Orange underside and long, forked tail are very different than those of most other swallows. Cliff and Cave Swallows may have some orange on underside, but are much smaller and lack a strongly forked tail.

DID YOU KNOW? Unmated males sometimes enter the nests of established breeding pairs, killing all of the nestlings. This allows the encroacher to then breed with the previously mated female, often producing a second, viable brood.

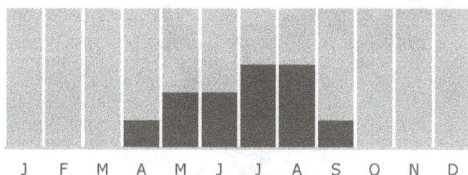

J F M A M J J A S O N D

163

② VEERY. *Catharus fuscescens.*

SIZE: 7 in.

HABITAT: Semi-dense woods, usually near a stream, wetland, or river. Sometimes prefers a thicketed understory.

WILD DIET: Insects (e.g., beetles, caterpillars), fruit (e.g., blueberries).

BEHAVIOR: Furtively probes through leaf litter with use of its bill, hopping along as it searches for insects and berries—the latter of which may also be obtained by directly gleaning from a branch. Occasionally takes flying insects out of the air with brief, deliberate flights. So named for its *veer* calls, which are down-slurred, metallic, and sometimes burbling.

MIGRATE? Yes.

NESTING: Selects a concealed location on or near the ground, amid brushy vegetation. Cup-shaped nest is constructed with leaves, bark, twigs, stems, and other plant fibers. About 6 in. across.

EGGS: Bright turquoise. Length of 1 in. Total of 3-4, sometimes with a second brood.

FEEDER BEHAVIOR: Does not visit feeders.

COMPARE TO SIMILAR SPECIES: Similar to other medium-sized thrushes, including the juvenile American Robin, the Wood Thrush, the Swainson's Thrush, and the Hermit Thrush (particularly the last two). The Veery has the least-spotted underside of those mentioned, with very light, almost indistinct tawny spotting on the upper breast. It also lacks a bold, white eye-ring like that of the Swainson's or Hermit.

DID YOU KNOW? Like many birds, the Veery varies its diet seasonally. During the breeding season, when more protein is often needed, this species primarily feeds on insects. Before and during migration, it instead consumes vast quantities of fruits and berries, providing an optimal energy source for long evening flights.

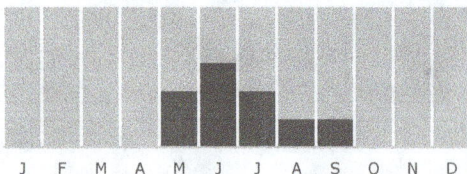

J F M A M J J A S O N D

Adult at top,
Adult at bottom (Photo by Andy Reago, Chrissy McClarren / CC BY-SA / Cropped).

Adults at top and bottom.

MEDIUM BIRDS (6 ½ - 8 ½")

① SWAINSON'S THRUSH. *Catharus ustulatus.*

SIZE: 7 in.

HABITAT: Dense, thicketed woods, usually near moving water. During migration, may be present in open woods, parks, and suburbs as well.

WILD DIET: Insects (e.g., beetles, caterpillars, flies), fruit (e.g., raspberries).

BEHAVIOR: Unlike most other spotted thrushes, this species customarily forages on elevated branches, rather than on the forest floor. It is often observed hopping along, occasionally lunging after an insect or craning its neck for ripe berries. With regard to the former, Swainson's Thrushes may also dive to the forest floor, hover, or sally out into the open for insects of interest. Its song is a quickly burbled, upward-spiraling series of chirps and flute-like notes.

MIGRATE? Yes.

NESTING: Selects a sheltered, concealed location in the fork or crotch of a shrub or low tree. Bulky, sloppy cup is woven of twigs, grasses, stems, and moss. About 5-6 in. across.

EGGS: Shades of turquoise, with light brown spotting. Length of 1 in. Total of 2-5.

FEEDER BEHAVIOR: Does not visit feeders.

COMPARE TO SIMILAR SPECIES: Similar to other medium-sized thrushes, including the juvenile American Robin, the Wood Thrush, the Veery, and the Hermit Thrush (particularly the last two). The Swainson's Thrush has more spotting on the breast than the Veery, and a much bolder, pale eye-ring. Compared to the Hermit Thrush, the Swainson's lacks a reddish tail, and has less profuse spotting on its underside.

DID YOU KNOW? Some ornithologists have suggested that the Western and Eastern populations of the Swainson's Thrush be subdivided into their own separate species. Individuals belonging to these populations are frequently labeled as Russet-backed and Olive-backed Thrushes, respectively.

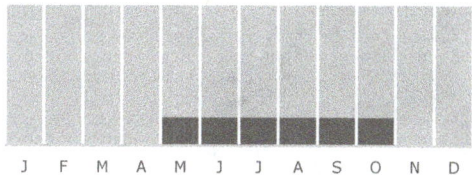

J F M A M J J A S O N D

167

① SEMIPALMATED PLOVER.
Charadrius semipalmatus.

SIZE: 7 in.

HABITAT: Mostly beaches and mudflats. During migration, this may include locations along a variety of smaller lakes, reservoirs, and even flooded fields; however, wintering sites are more strictly limited to oceanic coastlines. While found in pockets throughout Vermont, most common along the shores of Lake Champlain.

WILD DIET: Worms, aquatic invertebrates, and insects.

BEHAVIOR: This shorebird species is often observed in loose flocks, foraging along intertidal zones or mudflats for stranded worms and invertebrates. Individuals frenetically run, pause, and repeat as they scan for potential prey items—seldom wading into water more than an inch deep. The plovers peck in the direction of any movement in the substrate, with keen eyesight enabling the detection of worms and invertebrates up to a few inches below the surface. Call is a squeaky, rising *chweep*, which may also be uttered while foraging.

MIGRATE? Yes.

NESTING: Breeds along the tundra wetlands of northern Canada and Alaska. A very shallow nest scrape is made in the gravel, and lined with twigs and other vegetative debris. About 3 in. across.

EGGS: Off-white, with large dark spotting. Length of 1 ½ in. Total of 4.

FEEDER BEHAVIOR: Does not visit feeders.

COMPARE TO SIMILAR SPECIES: Similar to the much larger Killdeer, but has brighter orange legs, and only features one dark breast band (rather than two).

DID YOU KNOW? The Semipalmated Plover is named for the partial webbing present between its toes. This allows the plover to swim across narrow channels of water while foraging, though it seems to rarely employ this faculty—instead, normally taking short flights between feeding or roosting areas.

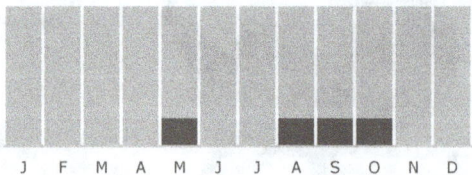

J F M A M J J A S O N D

Breeding adult at top (Note: This individual's legs have been banded for research pupuses),
Nonbreeding adult at bottom.

Breeding male at top,
Nonbreeding male at bottom left (in Sept. or Oct.),
Female at bottom right (Photo by Félix Uribe / CC BY-SA / Cropped).

② SCARLET TANAGER. *Piranga olivacea.*

SIZE: 7 in.

HABITAT: Dense, mature woods. During migration, also common in open woods, parks, and suburbs.

WILD DIET: Insects (e.g., ants, dragonflies, wasps) and spiders, sometimes fruit.

BEHAVIOR: This species of the treetops uses a variety of methods to capture its invertebrate prey. While foraging, Scarlet Tanagers have been known to walk along horizontal branches, vertically cling to bark, hover near flocks of flying insects, or even sally out with short, direct flights like a flycatcher. Up-and-down song is like that of an American Robin, but noticeably hoarser.

MIGRATE? Yes.

NESTING: Selects a high, sheltered location in the outer branches of a tree. Thick, sloppily constructed bowl of twigs and grasses. About 5 in. across.

EGGS: Pale blue-green, with light brown mottling. Length of 1 in. Total of 4.

BIRD FEEDING TIPS

FEEDER DIET: Fruit, grape jelly, mealworms, suet. **FEEDER TYPES**: Platforms. **FEEDER BEHAVIOR**: Uncommon, and normally only visits feeders during migration—particularly if there are insufficient numbers of insects (perhaps owing to a late spring).

COMPARE TO SIMILAR SPECIES: Most similar to the related Summer Tanager; males differ by way of their jet-black wings and tail, while females tend to be a much greener shade of yellow. Bright red coloration of males might also suggest a Northern Cardinal, though this cardinalid has a distinctive head crest and a frequently more upright posture.

DID YOU KNOW? This species has begun to experience increased nest failures near clearings and edges of woods, particularly due to the spread of the Brown-headed Cowbird, a fringe habitat specialist. This has contributed to the recent decline of tanager populations—an issue facing other regional songbirds as well.

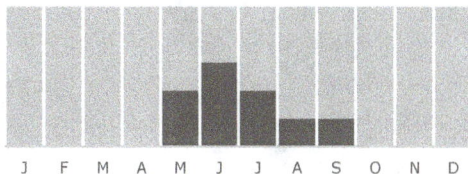

J F M A M J J A S O N D

171

① **BOBOLINK.** *Dolichonyx oryzivorus.*

SIZE: 7 in.
HABITAT: Overgrown fields and grasslands. Sometimes near wetlands.
WILD DIET: Seeds, insects and insect larvae, spiders, grains.
BEHAVIOR: A bird of meadows and prairies, this species is often found perched atop grassy stems, gleaning seeds from within the plant fibers. It also forages on the ground from time to time, particularly when taking insects and spiders. Both sexes are promiscuous with mating, and males are quite active when defending their territories, chasing rivals back and forth among the grasses. Emits a complex, liquid-like, and effervescent song, especially when in flight.
MIGRATE? Yes.
NESTING: Scrapes a depression in the ground amid a cover of dense vegetation. Finely woven bowl of dried grasses and stems. About 4 in. across.
EGGS: Light blue to rufous, with rusty mottling. Length of ¾ in. Total of 4-6.
FEEDER BEHAVIOR: Does not visit feeders.

COMPARE TO SIMILAR SPECIES: Males are very distinctive, especially in typical habitat. Females are plainer in color and thus may bear a passing resemblance to some grassland sparrows, but note that the female Bobolink is much larger and features a pale, beige underside.

DID YOU KNOW? Bobolinks are prodigious migrators, flying over 12,000 miles between northern North America and central South America twice yearly. Like many birds, this species is able to navigate by use of the Earth's magnetic field; in this case, magnetized iron oxides are present inside each bird's skull, closely bordering the olfactory nerves. This means that, loosely speaking, Bobolinks are able to actively *smell* their heading with specific reference to magnetic north and south.

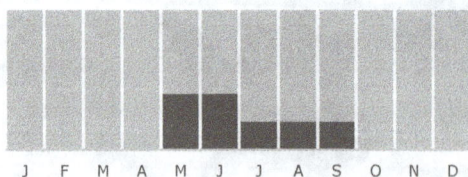

J F M A M J J A S O N D

Adult males at top and bottom left,
Adult females at bottom right.

Adult at top (Photo by Dominic Sherony / CC BY-SA / Cropped),
Adult at bottom (Photo by Kim Taylor Hull / CC BY-SA).

① **FOX SPARROW.** *Passerella iliaca.*

SIZE: 6 ¾ in.
HABITAT: Thicketed woods, brush, suburbs.
WILD DIET: Seeds, fruits, buds, insects and spiders.
BEHAVIOR: One of the first migrants to move north in the spring—and one of the last to return south in the fall—this plump, attractive sparrow prefers to inhabit brushy, obscured spots in the thicketed understory of woods. Like many larger sparrows and towhees, the Fox Sparrow tends to scratch-and-hop with both legs to uncover hidden tidbits from beneath debris. Song is an abbreviated melody of short chips and whistles.
MIGRATE? Yes.
NESTING: In the East, breeds mostly in Canada. Situated low in shrubs or evergreens, nest is a messy, thick cup of twigs and grasses. About 5-8 in. wide.
EGGS: Light blue-green, with thick brown mottling. Length of ¾ in. Total of 3-5.

BIRD FEEDING TIPS

FEEDER DIET: Black-oil and hulled sunflower seeds, cracked corn, millet, milo, nyjer, suet.
FEEDER TYPES: Ground, platforms. **FEEDER BEHAVIOR**: Known to conspicuously scrape-hop the ground with both legs to uncover fallen seeds. Not usually found together in large numbers, but may loosely associate with flocks of other sparrow species.

COMPARE TO SIMILAR SPECIES: Similar to Song Sparrow, but much larger with reddish-brown coloring. May also be confused with the similarly sized Hermit Thrush, but note the stouter, shorter bill and chunkier overall silhouette of the Fox Sparrow.

DID YOU KNOW? There are four distinct subspecies of the Fox Sparrow, each with separate geographies, differing physical characteristics, and distinct songs. These include the Red Fox Sparrow of central and eastern North America (pictured in all examples on the opposite page), the Sooty of the Pacific Coast, and the Slate-colored and Thick-billed of the interior West.

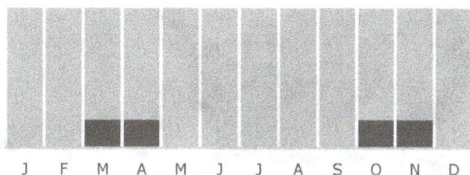

J F M A M J J A S O N D

(4) **WHITE-THROATED SPARROW.**
Zonotrichia albicollis.

SIZE: 6 ¾ in.

HABITAT: Thicketed woods, hedgerows, suburbs.

WILD DIET: Seeds (e.g., of grasses), fruits and berries, insects and spiders.

BEHAVIOR: Forages by hopping along the ground as it combs through leaf litter and vegetative debris. This species rummages for food by quickly scraping both feet along the ground, or by nudging away smaller items with the bill. May form somewhat large, loose flocks in some wintering territories. Song is a very distinctive, high-whistled *Oh-Can-a-da*, with the final three tones delivered at the same, higher pitch.

MIGRATE? Partially.

NESTING: Usually placed on the ground, sheltered beneath shrubs. Bowl is woven with fine grasses and stems. About 4 in. across.

EGGS: Off-white to light blue-green, with light brown splotching. Length of ¾ in. Total of 3-6, occasionally with a second brood.

BIRD FEEDING TIPS

FEEDER DIET: Black-oil and hulled sunflower seeds, cracked corn, millet, milo, suet. **FEEDER TYPES:** Ground, platforms. **FEEDER BEHAVIOR:** Relatively common visitor. Most often found on the ground as it forages for fallen seeds. May sometimes be outcompeted by other species of sparrows.

COMPARE TO SIMILAR SPECIES: Most similar to the White-crowned Sparrow, its close relative. Key differences include the White-throated's yellow spot in front of the eyes, as well as its namesake, bold-white throat.

DID YOU KNOW? On rare occasions, this species may nest aboveground in the branches of trees—but only if a first nest attempt has failed, normally due to predation. Common nest predators include grackles, jays, squirrels, and outdoor housecats.

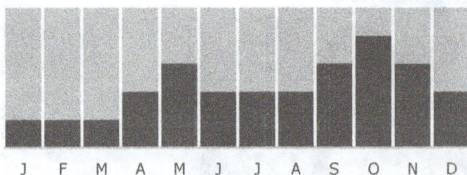

J F M A M J J A S O N D

Adults at top and bottom.

Adults at top and bottom.

② HERMIT THRUSH. *Catharus guttatus.*

SIZE: 6 ½ in.

HABITAT: Open woods, clearings of woods, thickets. Sometimes, walking paths and well-vegetated suburbs.

WILD DIET: Insects (e.g., beetles, caterpillars, flies), fruit (e.g., raspberries).

BEHAVIOR: This small species of thrush is most often located on the forest floor, where it alternatingly hops and pauses while foraging. The bill may be used to unsettle leaf litter in search of insects, and berries may be gleaned from bushes by stooping from a low branch. When perched, known to repeatedly cock its tail, before slowly relaxing downward. Song is a short, liquid series of woodwind-like tones, often described as one of the most exquisite of all birds'.

MIGRATE? Yes.

NESTING: Selects a hidden location low in a shrub or on the ground. Nest is a thick-lipped bowl, constructed mostly with dried grasses. About 4-6 in. across.

EGGS: Shades of light blue and turquoise, sometimes with light brown spotting. Length of 1 in. Total of 3-5. Usually raises 1-2 broods each year, but may sometimes attempt to hatch and raise a third.

FEEDER BEHAVIOR: Rarely visits feeders for mealworms or fruit.

COMPARE TO SIMILAR SPECIES: Similar to other medium-sized thrushes, including the juvenile American Robin, the Wood Thrush, the Veery, and the Swainson's Thrush (particularly the last two). The Hermit Thrush has darker and more profuse breast spotting than the Veery or Swainson's, and has a distinctive reddish-brown tail. In addition, it is smaller than the Wood Thrush, and lacks the Wood Thrush's clean, dark brown spotting across the breast *and* belly, and a reddish-brown back and head cap.

DID YOU KNOW? The Hermit Thrush is the only member of the spotted thrushes to winter in North America, rather than exclusively in Central or South America. Wintering territories include the American South, the Southwest, and the Pacific states, as well as most of Mexico.

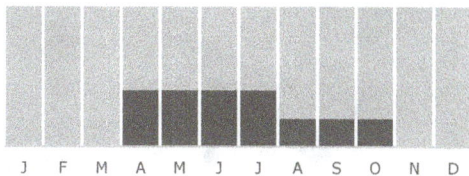

J F M A M J J A S O N D

④ **CEDAR WAXWING.** *Bombycilla cedrorum.*

SIZE: 6 ½ in.

HABITAT: Open woods, orchards, overgrown fields, and suburbs.

WILD DIET: Primarily fruit and berries. Also, some insects during breeding season.

BEHAVIOR: This frugivorous species is most often found wherever wild fruits and berries are available, and particularly amid the treetops. Forages for berries by hovering or stooping down from a branch; when pursuing insects, makes darting, agile flights from exposed perches. Congregates in medium to large-sized flocks, though some birds may wander a few hundred feet away near the fringes. Calls are repeated, high-pitched *tsee* notes.

MIGRATE? Partially.

NESTING: In a fork of tree branches, constructs a bowl of variable depth using woven twigs and grasses. About 5 in. across.

EGGS: Shades of blue-green, with dark spots. Length of ¾ in. Total of 4-7, occasionally with a second brood.

BIRD FEEDING TIPS

FEEDER DIET: Fruit. **FEEDER TYPES**: Platforms. **FEEDER BEHAVIOR**: Extremely uncommon at feeders, but likely to repeatedly visit yards with extensive plantings of native berry bushes and trees. However, do *not* plant the ornamental shrub *Nandina domestica*, also known as heavenly bamboo, as its berries are highly toxic to waxwings and other frugivorous (i.e., fruit-eating) birds.

COMPARE TO SIMILAR SPECIES: Closely resembles the Bohemian Waxwing, which is native to the evergreen forests of southern and central Canada, and may wander south in winters if there is an insufficient food supply. The Bohemian is much stouter, and has a grayish (rather than yellow) belly.

DID YOU KNOW? Waxwings are well-known for their habit of inadvertently consuming large quantities of overripe—and, therefore, fermenting—berries, a behavior which causes acute onset drunkenness. As a result, individuals may stagger about, fly repeatedly into cars and windows, and generally create a considerable hullabaloo.

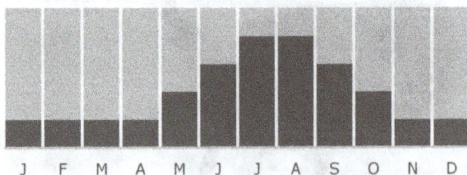

J F M A M J J A S O N D

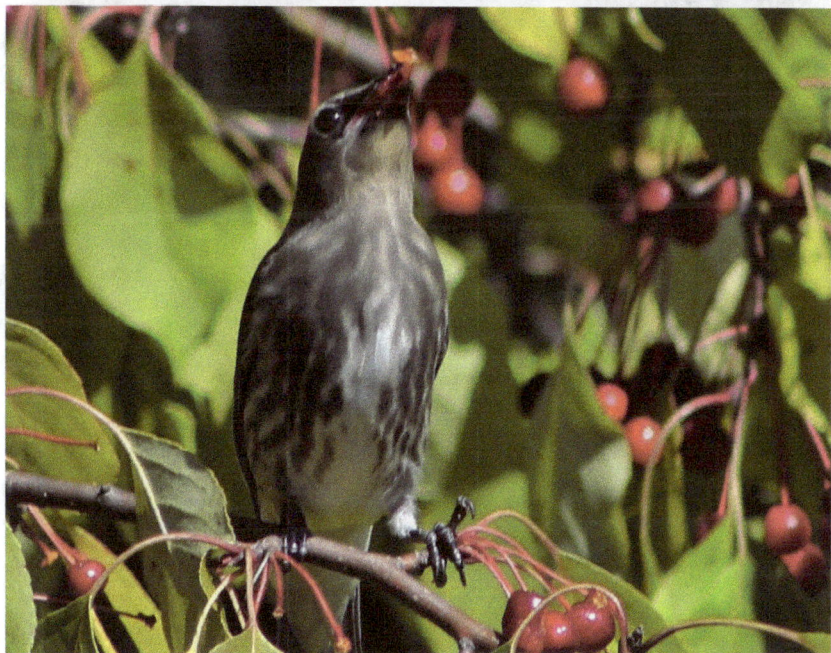

Adult at top,
Juvenile at bottom.

Adult at top,
Juvenile at bottom.

② **WHITE-CROWNED SPARROW.**
Zonotrichia leucophrys.

SIZE: 6 ½ in.

HABITAT: Thickets, overgrown fields, and suburbs.

WILD DIET: Seeds (e.g., of grasses), insects and spiders, berries, and grains.

BEHAVIOR: More active than some other sparrows, this handsome species hurriedly forages on the ground—moving by hopping, and displacing leaf litter by scratching the ground with both feet. Individuals are typically perched in brushy vegetation or on the ground, irregularly darting in and out of cover. This species' song is a cheerful mix of whistles, metallic rings, and trills, which varies regionally.

MIGRATE? Yes.

NESTING: Selects a concealed location amid the tangles of a shrub. Bowl of twigs, grasses, and stems with a messy outer rim. About 5 in. across.

EGGS: Shades of blue-green, with light brown mottling. Length of ¾ in. Total of 3-6, with 2-3 broods.

BIRD FEEDING TIPS

FEEDER DIET: Black-oil and hulled sunflower seeds, cracked corn, millet, milo, suet.
FEEDER TYPES: Ground, platforms. **FEEDER BEHAVIOR**: Ordinarily found on the ground, gleaning fallen seeds. May be accompanied by other species of sparrows.

COMPARE TO SIMILAR SPECIES: Most similar to the White-throated Sparrow, its close relative. Key differences include the White-throated's yellow spot in front of the eyes, as well as its namesake, bold white throat.

DID YOU KNOW? A group of field naturalists led by Elizabeth Derryberry found that this species' songs substantively increased in both clarity and overall range of pitch during the recent COVID-19 pandemic. This study took place in San Francisco, CA, with the cause thought to be reduced traffic noise.

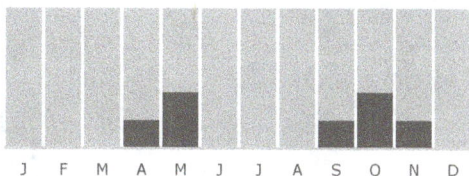

J F M A M J J A S O N D

⑤ **DOWNY WOODPECKER.** *Dryobates pubescens.*

SIZE: 6 ¼ in.

HABITAT: Open woods, suburbs.

WILD DIET: Mostly insects. Also, nuts (e.g., acorns), seeds, and berries.

BEHAVIOR: The smallest of the North American woodpeckers, this sparrow-sized bird is most often found industriously pecking away at tree bark. The beetles, ants, and larvae which are most often gleaned during this process constitute the majority of its diet, though this species is an exceedingly common backyard feeder visitor (particularly in winter). Commonly gives a high, squeaky *pic* call, and forms flocks much more readily than most other woodpecker species.

MIGRATE? No.

NESTING: Excavates a small cavity beneath a knob, often in a decaying tree. About 1 - 1 ½ in. across and 9 in. deep.

EGGS: White. Length of ¾ in. Total of 4-6, occasionally with a second brood.

BIRD FEEDING TIPS

FEEDER DIET: Suet, black-oil and hulled sunflower seeds, peanuts and peanut hearts, mealworms, safflower seed. **FEEDER TYPES:** Suet cages, hoppers, platforms, tubes. **FEEDER BEHAVIOR:** Acrobatically clings to hoppers or tubes, or pecks at suet cages. May arrive in small flocks if sufficient food sources available. During the breeding season, may be observed entertainingly chasing its conspecifics around and among the trees.

COMPARE TO SIMILAR SPECIES: Most similar to the larger Hairy Woodpecker, which is taller than the height of a standard suet cage. Downy has a bill shorter than the length of its head, and black spotting on its outer white tail feathers.

DID YOU KNOW? The Downy is a well-known predator of larvae of the invasive European corn borer, a moth which causes over $1 billion in yearly damages to the North American agricultural industry. This moth lays its eggs on the ears of corn, and larvae burrow into the crop as they rapidly mature and metamorphose.

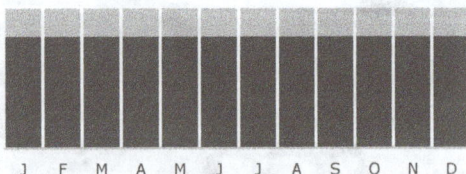

J F M A M J J A S O N D

Adult male at top (Notice red on back of head),
Adult female at bottom.

Adult male at top,
Adult female at bottom.

④ **HOUSE SPARROW.** *Passer domesticus.*

SIZE: 6 ¼ in.
HABITAT: Cities, suburbs, farms.
WILD DIET: Seeds, grains, garbage, insects and spiders.
BEHAVIOR: If sparrows are present on a sidewalk or flowerbed in any variety of urban environment, they are almost always members of this invasive species. House Sparrows tend to form large, noisy flocks, which feature surprisingly rigid hierarchical structures: older males have more black on the breast and throat, while younger individuals may tremulously flick their tails when approached by elders. Between foraging sessions, several dozen individuals may perch in nearby trees or bushes. Vocalizations are a mix of *chrip* and *churrip* notes.
MIGRATE? No.
NESTING: Often colonial. Uses natural and manmade cavities, such as tree hollows, eaves of houses, and dilapidated roofs. A tight cup of grasses and stems is lined with feathers, and may be adjacent to another nest. About 5 in. wide.
EGGS: Off-white to light blue-green, with brown speckling. Length of ¾ in. Total of 4-6. Raises 2-4 broods each year, usually 3.

BIRD FEEDING TIPS

FEEDER DIET: Black-oil and hulled sunflower seeds, millet, peanut hearts, cracked corn, milo, suet. **FEEDER TYPES**: Ground, platforms, hoppers, tubes. **FEEDER BEHAVIOR**: Often present in large, semi-localized flocks, which may overrun feeders. May claim, and even evict existing tenants of, nest boxes.

COMPARE TO SIMILAR SPECIES: Compared to New World sparrows and finches, the black throat and breast of male are distinctive. Generally, its habitat and chunky profile are the clearest giveaways, along with the presence of nearby, identifiable males.

DID YOU KNOW? House Sparrows, even if fully or partially blinded, are able to maintain a consistent circadian rhythm, owing to photoreceptors located inside the skull.

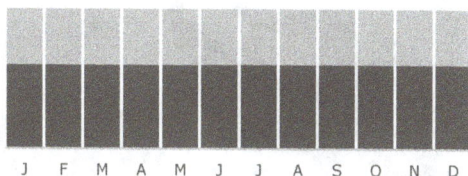

J F M A M J J A S O N D

④ **EASTERN PHOEBE.** *Sayornis phoebe.*

SIZE: 6 in.

HABITAT: Suburbs, open woods, field edges. Sometimes near sources of water.

WILD DIET: Flying insects. In colder months, may eat small fruits or berries.

BEHAVIOR: This dusky, solitary bird may initially seem unremarkable to passive observers; however, it is among the very first migrants to arrive in the spring, prominently perching on open branches while mirthfully bobbing its tail up and down. After frequent, darting flights out for prey, it almost always returns to the same perch, though it may select a new perch if insects are no longer present nearby. Its penchant for inhabiting open areas near houses, particularly during spring and fall migration, means that suburbanites will quickly grow familiar with this species' raspy, whistled *fee-bree*—repeated in tidy couplets all throughout the day.

MIGRATE? Yes.

NESTING: Prefers a rocky nook or cranny, often under manmade overhangs (e.g., eaves of roofs, fissures in concrete, etc.). Bowl of dried grasses and vegetation. About 6 in. across.

EGGS: Off-white to light pink, with mild speckling. Length of ¾ in. Total of 3-5, with 2 broods.

FEEDER BEHAVIOR: Does not normally visit feeders, though there have been rare reports of this species taking dried mealworms when food is scarce. May use nest boxes.

COMPARE TO SIMILAR SPECIES: The Eastern Wood-Pewee is of similar size and coloration. In particular, note the Eastern Phoebe's more slumped posture, darker head cap, and short, black bill.

DID YOU KNOW? Eastern Phoebes have successfully adapted their nesting habits to the ever-increasing presence of humankind, having previously used sheltered, rocky ledges. Some phoebes have even been observed nesting in the spaces vacated by fallen bricks in below-ground wells.

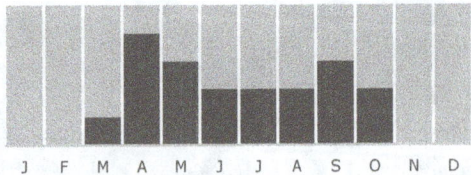

J F M A M J J A S O N D

Adult at top,
Juvenile at bottom (Notice light yellow on belly).

Adult male at top,
Adult female at bottom.

(5) **DARK-EYED JUNCO.** *Junco hyemalis.*

SIZE: 6 in.

HABITAT: Open to semi-open woods, thickets, parks, and suburbs.

WILD DIET: Mostly seeds, also insects and spiders.

BEHAVIOR: This species is most often associated with its flocking behavior during the winter months, when hosts of up to several dozen drip from the trees and populate clearings on the ground—all the while singing with soft, sweet, whistled trills. At foraging sites with ample resources, other species of sparrows may associate with juncos, forming busy, mixed flocks. Females tend to winter farther south than many males, as they are socially subordinate given their slightly smaller size. Like many small, flocking birds, this species tends to be a prime target for Cooper's and Sharp-shinned Hawks, which may monitor suburban feeders with particularly well-established avian denizens.

MIGRATE? Partially.

NESTING: Selects a concealed, brushy depression in the ground. Cup-shaped nest is finely woven of grasses. About 5 in. across.

EGGS: Off-white to light blue, with various brown markings. Length of ¾ in. Total of 3-5, with 2 broods.

BIRD FEEDING TIPS

FEEDER DIET: Millet, milo, black-oil and hulled sunflower seeds, nyjer, peanut hearts, cracked corn, safflower seed, suet. **FEEDER TYPES**: Ground, platforms, hoppers, tubes. **FEEDER BEHAVIOR**: Gathers in rather large, peaceable flocks. When arriving, tends to aerially dart from a nearby tree or shrub, descending to the ground beneath the feeders.

COMPARE TO SIMILAR SPECIES: Very much a *sui generis*, two-toned sparrow.

DID YOU KNOW? There are six separate North American subspecies of junco, each of which was formerly classified as its own species. The Slate-colored taxon is pictured, and is the only common variety in this region. However, the brown-sided Oregon Junco may arrive as a vagrant from its typical westerly range, and is known to flock with Slate-coloreds in such cases.

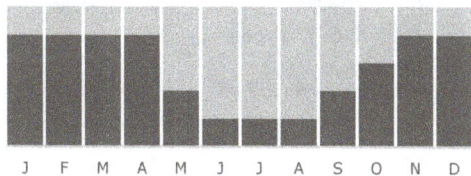

J F M A M J J A S O N D

③ **AMERICAN TREE SPARROW.**

Spizelloides arborea.

SIZE: 6 in.

HABITAT: Overgrown fields, edges of wetlands, open woods, and suburbs.

WILD DIET: Seeds (e.g., of grasses), berries, insects and spiders.

BEHAVIOR: The American Tree Sparrow's name is a certifiable misnomer, with individuals ordinarily found foraging near the ground in weedy or brushy areas. This species hops along as it busily gleans fallen seeds and low-hanging berries, with insects and spiders only a significant part of the diet during the summer months. When foraging, may emit brief, chattering calls.

MIGRATE? Yes.

NESTING: Breeds in northern Canada and Alaska, in tundra scrub. Nest is a grassy cup on the ground, partly hidden by surrounding vegetation and lined with grouse feathers. About 4-5 in. across.

EGGS: Shades of blue-green, with brown speckling. Length of ¾ in. Total of 4-6.

BIRD FEEDING TIPS

FEEDER DIET: Millet, black-oil and hulled sunflower seeds, nyjer, milo, peanut hearts, cracked corn, suet. **FEEDER TYPES**: Ground, platforms, hoppers, tubes. **FEEDER BEHAVIOR**: Semi-frequent visitor during the cold winter months, usually in small groups.

COMPARE TO SIMILAR SPECIES: Similar to Field and Chipping Sparrows, but noticeably larger and plumper than both. Also, notice its characteristic, dark breast spot and bicolored bill.

DID YOU KNOW? A group of sparrows is frequently called a host, crew, or meinie (e.g., a host of sparrows).

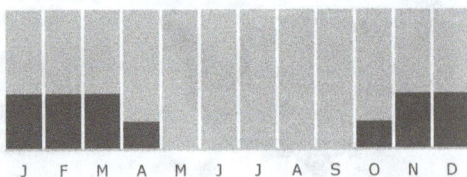

J F M A M J J A S O N D

Adults at top and bottom.

Adults at top and bottom.

④ TUFTED TITMOUSE. *Baeolophus bicolor.*

SIZE: 6 in.

HABITAT: Dense woods, wooded parks, and suburbs.

WILD DIET: Insects (e.g., caterpillars, wasps) and spiders, nuts (e.g., acorns), seeds, berries.

BEHAVIOR: A lively, nimble bird of the forests, this species restlessly flits from branch to branch: only taking fitful spells of rest when plotting its next foraging expeditions. Titmice are known to store seeds and nuts in the interstices of tree bark during fall and winter, often shelling them beforehand to allow for easy meals in the colder days ahead. Individuals also tend to select the largest seeds that will fit in their beaks, and peck them apart while pinning them to a perch with their feet. Song is a pellucid, high-whistled series of *pe-ter, pe-ter, pe-ter*, and calls include nasal buzzes and rasps similar to those of chickadees.

MIGRATE? No.

NESTING: Cavity nester. Uses tree hollows and former woodpecker nests, as well as small manmade cavities. A messy cup of grasses, mosses, and occasionally snake skins is constructed inside, and lined with animal hairs. About 4 in. wide.

EGGS: Off-white, with red or brown speckling. Length of ¾ in. Total of 3-8, sometimes with a second brood.

BIRD FEEDING TIPS

FEEDER DIET: Black-oil and hulled sunflower seeds, peanuts and peanut hearts, safflower seed, suet, mealworms. **FEEDER TYPES**: Platforms, hoppers, tubes, suet cages. **FEEDER BEHAVIOR**: Rarely stays for more than a few seconds during each visit, quickly finding a choice tidbit to store or consume nearby. When just one is observable, several more are usually nearby: forming loose, social groups known as troupes or banditries. Also, may use nest boxes.

COMPARE TO SIMILAR SPECIES: Black-crested Titmouse of Texas has a conspicuous, isolated dark crest. Much smaller and paler than Eastern Bluebird, with a fully white underside.

DID YOU KNOW? With the help of bird feeders, this species has expanded its original, more southerly range to include much of the Great Lakes and Northeast.

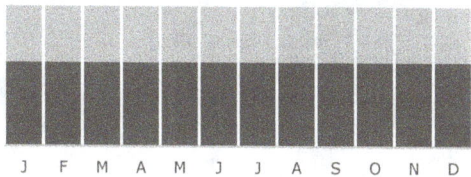

| J | F | M | A | M | J | J | A | S | O | N | D |

⑤ SONG SPARROW. *Melospiza melodia.*

SIZE: 5 ¾ in.

HABITAT: Thickets, hedgerows, overgrown fields, wetlands, open woods, parks. Very common in suburbs.

WILD DIET: Seeds (e.g., of grasses), fruits and berries, grains, insects and spiders.

BEHAVIOR: The most common sparrow across much of North America, this small, streaked species is ordinarily found skulking about brushy sections of habitat. In spring, the male spectacularly sings from exposed perches in bushes and small trees, with more exacting refrains preferred by potential female mates. Song is a sweet, multi-phrase melody of chips, whistles, buzzes, and trills.

MIGRATE? Partially.

NESTING: Usually placed on the ground in brushy or grassy areas, sometimes in a garden. Nest is cup-shaped, and woven with fine grasses. About 5-7 in. wide.

EGGS: Shades of blue-green, with brown speckling. Length of ¾ in. Total of 2-5, with 2-3 broods.

BIRD FEEDING TIPS

FEEDER DIET: Millet, milo, black-oil and hulled sunflower seeds, nyjer, peanut hearts, cracked corn, safflower seed, suet. **FEEDER TYPES:** Ground, platforms, hoppers, tubes. **FEEDER BEHAVIOR:** Very common on the ground beneath feeders, where it may take refuge in nearby cover between foraging sessions. Well-planted yards usually attract more individuals.

COMPARE TO SIMILAR SPECIES: Very similar to the Savannah Sparrow, which is instead found in open fields. May also resemble the Lincoln's Sparrow, which has a bolder topmost head stripe and a yellow tinge to the breast. Compared to female House and Purple Finches, this species has cleaner underside streaking and a less stout bill.

DID YOU KNOW? Song Sparrows successfully diminish the risks of predation and cowbird parasitism on their ground-based nests by laying several clutches of eggs throughout the late spring and summer.

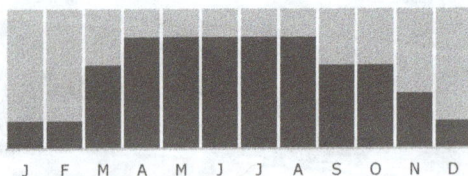

J F M A M J J A S O N D

Adults at top and bottom.

Adult male at top,
Adult female at bottom (Photo by Fyn Kynd / CC BY-SA / Cropped).

③ **PURPLE FINCH.** *Haemorhous purpureus.*

SIZE: 5 ¾ in.
HABITAT: Variety of woods, but favors conifers. Also, suburbs.
WILD DIET: Seeds, buds, berries, and insects.
BEHAVIOR: This cranberry-hued species actively forages by gleaning seeds and berries from foliage, occasionally landing on the ground to investigate fallen items of interest. Hops, rather than walks: like most other small finches and sparrows.
MIGRATE? Partially.
NESTING: Selects a sheltered spot in the outer branches of a tree, usually an evergreen. Cup-shaped, and woven with twigs and fine grasses. About 6-8 in. across.
EGGS: Light turquoise, with light brown speckling. Length of ¾ in. Total of 3-5, with 1-2 broods.

BIRD FEEDING TIPS

FEEDER DIET: Black-oil and hulled sunflower seeds, millet, nyjer, suet. **FEEDER TYPES:** Platforms, ground, hoppers, tubes. **FEEDER BEHAVIOR:** May join larger flocks of House Finches. Substantial plantings of evergreens help to further attract this species.

COMPARE TO SIMILAR SPECIES: Purple Finch males have little to no streaking on the lower belly and have darker red coloration that runs from the head *into the wings and back*; females have *a pronounced pale eyebrow*. By contrast, House Finches generally have a dirtier, more heavily streaked lower belly and a more shallowly forked tail; in addition, males have no red on the wings and females lack well-defined striping across the side of head. Sparrows generally have daintier bills.

DID YOU KNOW? Though Purple Finches are only ordinarily found in the northern states and in Canada, they are known to irrupt southward across the U.S. during years of evergreen cone scarcity. In exceptional cases, it is likely that this species may even venture into Mexico in search of adequate food sources.

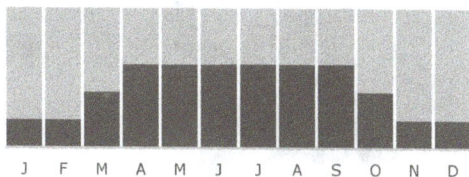

J F M A M J J A S O N D

② EASTERN WOOD-PEWEE. *Contopus virens.*

SIZE: 5 ½ in.

HABITAT: Variety of woods, but most frequently open, deciduous woods or edges of woods.

WILD DIET: Insects. Rarely, small fruits and berries.

BEHAVIOR: Selects elevated, well-visible perches from which to repeatedly sally out into the open for flying insects (e.g., dragonflies, wasps), occasionally stooping to vegetation or near the ground for wingless insects. Returns to the same perch after each flight; if an insect has been caught, it is repeatedly bludgeoned against the perch until it has been readied for consumption. Often hunts in the mid-canopy, beneath the domain of the Great Crested Flycatcher, but above that of the Least Flycatcher. Well-known for its ascending, high-whistled *pee-a-weee* call, which is sometimes audible for hundreds of feet.

MIGRATE? Yes.

NESTING: Nests at the confluence of several branches, about 30-60 ft. high. Finely woven cup of dried grasses and plant fibers. About 2 in. across.

EGGS: Off-white, with some rufous speckling. Length of ¾ in. Total of 2-4.

FEEDER BEHAVIOR: Does not visit feeders.

COMPARE TO SIMILAR SPECIES: To separate from *Empidonax* flycatchers, note that this species returns frequently to the same, conspicuous perch, and seldom flicks its tail. Possesses more defined white wing bars and an often sleeker silhouette than the Eastern Phoebe. Overall, characteristic song is highly diagnostic, especially when distinguishing from the Western Wood-Pewee in the Great Plains states.

DID YOU KNOW? Male wood-pewees aggressively defend a breeding territory of about 10 acres, and sometimes father two nests—each with a different female.

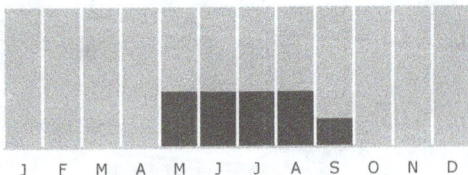

J F M A M J J A S O N D

Adults at top and bottom.

Male at top,
Female at bottom.

SMALL TO MEDIUM BIRDS (5 ½ - 6 ½")

④ **HOUSE FINCH.** *Carpodacus mexicanus*.

SIZE: 5 ½ in.
HABITAT: Cities and suburbs, open woods.
WILD DIET: Grains, seeds, and berries.
BEHAVIOR: Forages for food on the ground or in shrubbery, and perches in trees. Readily adapts to human habitation, often flocking in the vicinity of known feeders. Sings with complex, warbling melodies; calls with a sharp, ascending, and yanking tone.
MIGRATE? No.
NESTING: Openings in buildings, in shrubs or trees, or in outdoor décor. Cup-shaped; formed from small twigs and debris. About 6 in. across, and often 5-10 ft. above the ground.
EGGS: Off-white to light blue or green, with some dark speckling. Length of ¾ in. Total of 3-5, with 2-3 broods.

BIRD FEEDING TIPS

FEEDER DIET: Black-oil and hulled sunflower seeds, nyjer, safflower seed, suet. **FEEDER TYPES**: Platforms, ground, hoppers, tubes. **FEEDER BEHAVIOR**: Can accumulate in flocks of several dozen, jostling for position but remaining present for several minutes or more. May outcompete other species when found in sufficient numbers.

COMPARE TO SIMILAR SPECIES: Purple Finch males have little to no streaking on the lower belly and have darker red coloration that runs from the head into wings and back; females have a pronounced pale eyebrow. By contrast, House Finches generally have a dirtier, more heavily streaked lower belly and a more shallowly forked tail; in addition, males have *no red on the folded wings* and females *lack well-defined striping across the side of head*. Sparrows generally have daintier bills.

DID YOU KNOW? House Finches are only native to the western half of the U.S. Following illegal sales in the pet trade during the 1940s, they colonized the entire eastern U.S., working their way westward from New York City before finally reuniting with their relatives near the Rocky Mountains around the year 2000.

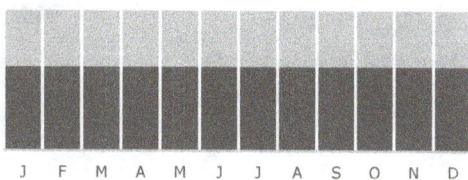

J F M A M J J A S O N D

① LEAST SANDPIPER. *Calidris minutilla.*

SIZE: 5 ½ in.

HABITAT: Mudflats on edges of lakes, rivers, ponds, wetlands, and flooded fields.

WILD DIET: Insects and insect larvae, as well as very small aquatic invertebrates (e.g., snails).

BEHAVIOR: Probes the mud for small prey items buried in the substrate. Though it prefers mudflats, it also enters the inch-deep shallows of nearby water. Found in small to medium-sized groups, and may flock with other similarly sized shorebirds. Easily flushed if approached too closely, with individuals taking a somewhat direct path to another nearby foraging site. Along with the Spotted Sandpiper, this species is among the most common of all inland shorebirds.

MIGRATE? Yes.

NESTING: Breeds in the far north of Canada and Alaska. Forms a cuplike depression among stalks of thick grasses. About 2-3 in. across.

EGGS: Off-white with brown mottling. Length of 1 in. Total of 3-4.

FEEDER BEHAVIOR: Does not visit feeders.

COMPARE TO SIMILAR SPECIES: Other small "peep" sandpipers are often similar, but the Least is smallest and has *yellow legs.* Among breeding adults, the brown of its folded wings, back, and head cap is darker than that of the Semipalmated Sandpiper. Nonbreeding adults have a buffy band across the entire width of the breast and feature a darker gray-brown back, unlike the pale gray of the Western Sandpiper or the medium gray of the Semipalmated.

DID YOU KNOW? Though the smallest shorebird in the world, some individuals of this species have been known to undertake nonstop migratory flights exceeding 2,000 miles.

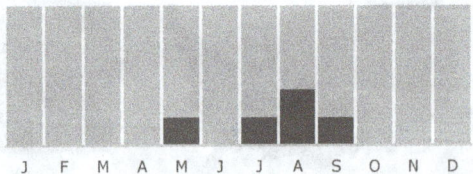

J F M A M J J A S O N D

Breeding adults at top,
Nonbreeding adults at bottom.

Breeding adult at top,
Nonbreeding adult at bottom.

④ CHIPPING SPARROW. *Spizella passerina.*

SIZE: 5 ½ in.

HABITAT: Open woods, parks, cities and suburbs.

WILD DIET: Seeds (e.g., of dandelions, wild buckwheat), insects and spiders.

BEHAVIOR: This spirited sparrow of the suburbs is ubiquitous in its favored habitat: hopping along near edges of lawns, perching in trees and shrubs, and gathering in small, loose flocks near feeders. Often prefers to perch between foraging sessions in sheltered, dense evergreens, if available. Song is a series of chipped, almost insect-like trills, which lasts up to five or six seconds.

MIGRATE? Yes.

NESTING: Selects a chest-high fork of branches in a shrub or tree, usually an evergreen. Height may be as low as one foot—or as high as 15 feet—above the ground. A cup is woven of twigs, grasses, and rootlets. About 5 in. across.

EGGS: Light blue or off-white, with brown spotting. Length of ¾ in. Total of 2-6, with 2 broods.

BIRD FEEDING TIPS

FEEDER DIET: Millet, milo, nyjer, hulled sunflower seeds, suet. **FEEDER TYPES**: Hoppers, tubes, platforms, ground. **FEEDER BEHAVIOR**: Very common feeder visitor, and may also nest in a backyard tree or hedgerow. Gathers for moderate periods on smaller feeders, and may also loiter on the ground if fallen seed is present.

COMPARE TO SIMILAR SPECIES: During the breeding season, this species' rufous crest resembles that of the Field Sparrow, but note the black eyeline and long, white eyebrow of the Chipping (in addition to the fact that the Field is more common in open, rural grasslands).

DID YOU KNOW? Like many other birds, this species migrates by night—and, in fact, ranks as one of the most common such migrants. Ornithological sound technicians have been able to deduce species frequency patterns at a given site by counting nocturnal flight calls; usually, about 10 brief, high-pitched chips per hour can be easily heard for this species, and occasionally over 150 Chipping Sparrows per hour are logged.

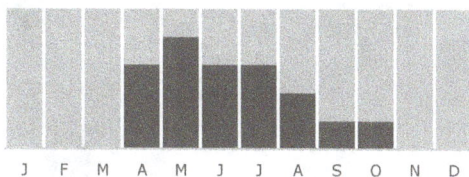

J F M A M J J A S O N D

③ RED-EYED VIREO. *Vireo olivaceus.*

SIZE: 5 ½ in.

HABITAT: Mature, old-growth, usually deciduous woods. During migration, also in open woods, parks, and suburbs.

WILD DIET: Mostly insects (e.g., caterpillars, flies) and spiders, but also fruits and berries (particularly before and during migration).

BEHAVIOR: This prodigious melodist is capable of generating numerous ditties over the course of a day, usually from high in a mature, deciduous tree. Individuals tend to move more purposefully than many of the warblers and kinglets, with short investigatory hops along the branches of the canopy. Smaller insects are quickly snapped up, while caterpillars and grasshoppers may be pinned to the perch with one claw while consumed piecemeal. Occasionally, vireos may hover near the tips of branches to capture elusive insects on the undersides of foliage. Songs consist of short, up-and-down series of chirped or murmured notes, often repeated after a rest of no more than a few seconds.

MIGRATE? Yes.

NESTING: Selects a location in a deciduous tree, with branches or twigs forming part of the nest's rim. Nest hangs from these anchor points, and is partially suspended in midair. Woven with grasses and twigs, and thoroughly bound with spider webbing. About 3 in. across.

EGGS: White, with fine spotting. Length of ¾ in. Total of 2-4, with 1-2 broods.

FEEDER BEHAVIOR: Does not visit feeders.

COMPARE TO SIMILAR SPECIES: Very similar to other vireo species, such as the Warbling and Philadelphia. Note the dark-outlined, clearly defined pale eyebrow, which is most prominent in the Red-eyed, as well as the contrast between its grey head cap and light green back.

DID YOU KNOW? Red-eyed Vireos may sing as many as 50 distinct songs, and rarely cease vocalizing: with some birds singing over 20,000 times in a single day.

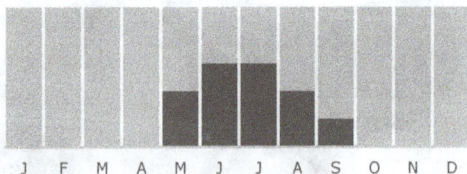

J F M A M J J A S O N D

Adults at top and bottom.

Adult male at top (Note the black—rather than gray—cap),
Adult female at bottom.

⑤ WHITE-BREASTED NUTHATCH.
Sitta carolinensis.

SIZE: 5 ¼ in.

HABITAT: Mature woods, either open or dense. Also, parks and suburbs.

WILD DIET: Insects (e.g., ants, larvae, caterpillars) and spiders, seeds and nuts.

BEHAVIOR: Nuthatches are often observed clinging upside-down to tree bark, periodically extending their heads outward to survey their surroundings. Short, firm hops allow individuals to descend the tree trunk or cling to branches, often in search of insects (in the summer) or seeds and nuts (winter). Throughout the colder months, often observed in larger mixed flocks with titmice and chickadees, which assist with locating food sources and maintaining a vigil for lurking predators: particularly Cooper's and Sharp-shinned Hawks. Also known for its raucous, nasally, and cackling *ha-a-a-a...* calls, which may echo for hundreds of feet.

MIGRATE? No, but short movements may sometimes occur in winter.

NESTING: Cavity nester. Uses natural tree hollows or former woodpecker nests, which can be rather more commodious than one might expect. A bowl of grasses and bark is lined with feathers. About 4-5 in. across.

EGGS: White, with russet spotting. Length of ¾ in. Total of 3-8.

BIRD FEEDING TIPS

FEEDER DIET: Black-oil and hulled sunflower seeds, peanuts and peanut hearts, suet, mealworms, safflower seed. **FEEDER TYPES**: Tubes, hoppers, suet cages, platforms. **FEEDER BEHAVIOR**: A series of brief visits allows this species to take large seeds and nuts, before pecking them apart (or "hatching" them) in the cranny of a tree; these may also be stored in bark crevices in late fall and winter. Also, sometimes uses nest boxes.

COMPARE TO SIMILAR SPECIES: Red-breasted Nuthatch is very similar, but has a dark black eyeline and orange underside. Chickadees may also resemble this species, but note the distinct differences in movement (i.e., rarely upside down).

DID YOU KNOW? Nuthatches roost alone in tree cavities; however, in very cold weather, up to a couple dozen may crowd together in a single roost for warmth.

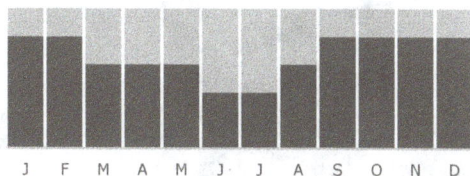

J F M A M J J A S O N D

② CHIMNEY SWIFT. *Chaetura pelagica.*

SIZE: 5 ¼ in.

HABITAT: Cities and suburbs, parks, and fields.

WILD DIET: Flying insects (e.g., flies, ants, beetles, wasps).

BEHAVIOR: Usually described as a "cigar with wings," this diminutive bird spends the entire day in the air. Low wing-loading allows for seemingly effortless flight: with alternating gliding and flitting of wings, and calls which resound with a barrage of chittering. May reach diving speeds of well over 100 mph, and typically observed at speeds of 30 to 75 mph in level flight. During breeding season, most swifts stay relatively close to colonial nest sites, though individuals may venture up to five miles away. Swifts are unable to perch, and exclusively cling vertically to hard surfaces at their roosting or nesting sites, which include the interiors of chimneys and hollowed-out tree trunks.

MIGRATE? Yes.

NESTING: Previously nested in caves and hollowed tree trunks; now, almost exclusively nests in uncovered chimney flues. Bowl of twigs is bound together and to the vertical surface with cement-like saliva. About 4 in. across.

EGGS: Bright white. Length of ¾ in. Total of 3-5.

FEEDER BEHAVIOR: Does not visit feeders.

COMPARE TO SIMILAR SPECIES: Short, stubby body and very long, narrow wings differentiate from various swallows and nightjars. Unlike bats, this species normally flies by light of day.

DID YOU KNOW? Particularly during migration, flocks of thousands of swifts often descend to a communal roost, such as a chimney or smokestack, en masse. This results in an enormous, funnel-like conglomeration which ranks among the most enrapturing spectacles in all of urban birdwatching.

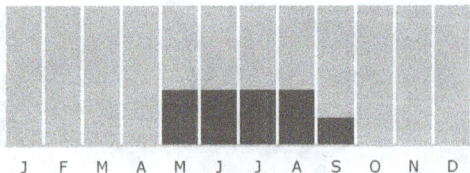

J F M A M J J A S O N D

Adults at top and bottom.

Adult male at top,
Adult female at bottom left (Photo by Andrew Weitzel / CC BY-SA / Cropped),
Juvenile at bottom right.

② **YELLOW-RUMPED WARBLER.**
Setophaga coronata.

SIZE: 5 ¼ in.

HABITAT: Open to semi-open woods. In winter, also suburbs, parks, and dunes.

WILD DIET: Mostly insects (e.g., beetles, caterpillars, aphids) and spiders. In winter, also fruits and berries (e.g., bayberry, juniper, poison ivy).

BEHAVIOR: An adaptable and varied forager, this species is known to plunder spider webs, catch flying insects which pass too close to an exposed perch, and cling to and probe the bark of trees—in addition to more customary warbler foraging habitats, such as hopping along and exploring branches. In winter, this species may consume copious amounts of berries, allowing it to stay much farther north than many other warblers. Song is a simple, burbling series.

MIGRATE? Yes.

NESTING: Selects a location atop a cluster of conifer branches. Twigs, grasses, and needles are used to loosely weave a cup-shaped nest. About 3-4 in. across.

EGGS: Off-white, with brown speckling. Length of ¾ in. Total of 3-5, occasionally with a second brood.

BIRD FEEDING TIPS

FEEDER DIET: Suet, mealworms, fruit, grape jelly, sugar water, black-oil and hulled sunflower seeds, peanut hearts. **FEEDER TYPES:** Hoppers, tubes, platforms, suet cages, nectar feeders, ground. **FEEDER BEHAVIOR:** An uncommon feeder visitor, this species is most likely to visit during migration or in winter. May be otherwise common in the backyard.

COMPARE TO SIMILAR SPECIES: Most similar to Magnolia and Yellow-throated Warblers. The Yellow-rumped has a conspicuous black mask, yellow rump, white belly (unlike the yellow belly of the Magnolia) and band of streaking across the breast (unlike the fully yellow throat and breast of the Yellow-throated).

DID YOU KNOW? The Yellow-rumped Warbler is split into two North American subspecies, the Myrtle and the Audubon's. Myrtle Warblers are as pictured, and are more common east of the Rockies; while the Audubon's features a yellow (rather than white) throat, and is more common near the Rockies and in the West.

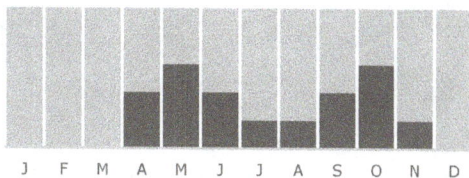

J F M A M J J A S O N D

⑤ BLACK-CAPPED CHICKADEE.
Poecile atricapillus.

SIZE: 5 ¼ in.

HABITAT: Various woods, parks, and suburbs.

WILD DIET: Insects (caterpillars, larvae) and spiders, seeds, nuts, and berries.

BEHAVIOR: This high-spirited species is normally found in loose flocks, acrobatically clinging to branches while gleaning hard-to-reach foodstuffs. Insects are taken in short flights or directly from vegetation. Upon securing a nut or seed and flying to a secure perch, the object is pinned against a branch with the feet and broken with the bill. Call is a well-known *chick-a-dee-dee...*, with the number of *dees* increasing with the relative level of perceived danger.

MIGRATE? No.

NESTING: Cavity nesters, often using a self-excavated hollow. Inside, a cup is arranged of grasses, and lined with animal hair. Interior nest is about 4 in. wide.

EGGS: White, with reddish-brown spotting. Length of ½ in. Total of 3-8.

BIRD FEEDING TIPS

FEEDER DIET: Black-oil and hulled sunflower seeds, peanuts and peanut hearts, suet, mealworms, safflower seed, nyjer. **FEEDER TYPES**: Platforms, hoppers, tubes, suet cages. **FEEDER BEHAVIOR**: Visits for no more than 10 seconds, and usually shorter—preferring to hull and consume seeds from nearby perch. Inquisitive. Occasionally uses nest boxes.

COMPARE TO SIMILAR SPECIES: The uncommon Boreal Chickadee, which is occasionally present in the northern half of the state, has a brown cap and tawny flanks.

DID YOU KNOW? Like titmice, a group of chickadees is known as a banditry: owing either to their vaguely felonious black masks, or their snatch-and-grab feeding behavior.

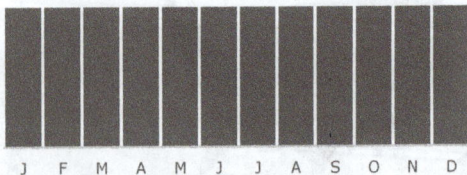

J F M A M J J A S O N D

Adults at top and bottom.

Breeding male at top,
Nonbreeding male at bottom left,
Female at bottom right.

② **INDIGO BUNTING.** *Passerina cyanea.*

SIZE: 5 ¼ in.

HABITAT: Mostly thickets and overgrown fields. Sometimes, edges of woods and roadsides; during migration, also suburbs, meadows, and open woods.

WILD DIET: Insects, seeds, berries, and grains.

BEHAVIOR: Forages low or along the ground in thickets, variably clinging to unstable stems and grasses as it cranes its neck to reach potential food sources. Normally found solitarily or in very small groups, aside from during migration. When singing (sometimes from elevated perches), note its high-pitched, coupled *whip, whip* or *chew, chew*, which forms the basis of longer melodic stanzas.

MIGRATE? Yes.

NESTING: Low to the ground, in a fork of dense vegetation. Cup-shaped, woven with grasses, and wrapped with spider webbing. About 2-3 in. across.

EGGS: White, sometimes with light brown spotting. Length of ¾ in. Total of 3-4, with 2 broods.

BIRD FEEDING TIPS

FEEDER DIET: Nyjer, millet, mealworms, milo, black-oil and hulled sunflower seeds, oats. **FEEDER TYPES:** Ground, tubes, hoppers, platforms. **FEEDER BEHAVIOR:** Most likely to visit in migration: sporadically in flocks of up to several dozen. Otherwise, uncommon.

COMPARE TO SIMILAR SPECIES: Key year-round differences from the Lazuli Bunting of western North America (which, consequently, is very rare in New England) include an absence of orange on the male's breast, and the lack of distinct wing bars on the female. The regionally uncommon Blue Grosbeak is also similar in appearance, but is larger and has a much stouter bill.

DID YOU KNOW? Indigo Buntings are the Galileans of the avian kingdom. During migration, which is undertaken by night, individuals accurately navigate by referencing the positions of the stars, even adjusting as constellations move over the course of weeks, seasons, and years. Indeed, captive buntings are even known to experience confusion if deprived of the ability to see the celestial lights.

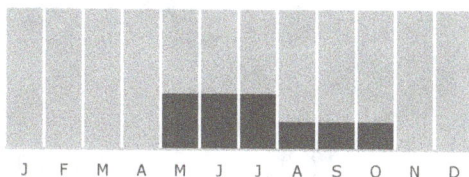

J F M A M J J A S O N D

② **YELLOW WARBLER.** *Setophaga petechia.*

SIZE: 5 ¼ in.

HABITAT: Thicketed woods near rivers, streams, and wetlands. Also, parks and suburbs, particularly during migration.

WILD DIET: Insects (e.g., caterpillars, beetles) and spiders.

BEHAVIOR: This brightly appointed warbler is most at home in and around wet thickets, hopping along branches as it gleans insects. Like other warblers, this species is fairly active, frequently moving from branch to branch as it forages. Song is a cheerful, whistled *sweet-sweet-sweet-sweet, I'm so-so-sweet.*

MIGRATE? Yes.

NESTING: Selects a deep fork of a shrub or tree. A cup-shaped nest is woven of grasses and stems, and extensively bound with spider webbing. The nest is lined with feathers or downy pollen. About 3-4 in. across.

EGGS: Off-white to light blue-green, with brown spotting. Length of ¾ in. Total of 3-5.

FEEDER BEHAVIOR: Rarely visits feeders.

COMPARE TO SIMILAR SPECIES: Compared to other similar warblers, such as the Orange-crowned, this species is the only one which is so uniformly bright yellow. In addition, the male features distinctive red streaking on the breast.

DID YOU KNOW? The Yellow Warbler is one of the only avian species which consistently recognizes and defends against the threat of Brown-headed Cowbirds, with a specialized alert call often given if one is noticed nearby. Furthermore, if a cowbird lays eggs in the warbler's nest, a new nest will be immediately constructed atop the former one: smothering the mixed nest. If this is repeated several times over the course of the breeding season, a multi-story stack of nests may even emerge.

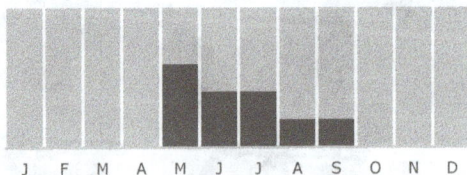

J F M A M J J A S O N D

Adult male at top,
Adult female at bottom.

Adults at top and bottom.

④ TREE SWALLOW. *Tachycineta bicolor.*

SIZE: 5 in.

HABITAT: Fields, wetlands, and lakes.

WILD DIET: Mostly flying insects (e.g., dragonflies, ladybugs), sometimes egg shells and fish bones before egg-laying for added calcium. During cold snaps in its wintering range, may resort to consuming bayberries as well.

BEHAVIOR: Often observed perching on wires, branches, or fence posts, this species is common across its preferred habitat in most of North America. The Tree Swallow forages by gliding somewhat low over the ground, with occasional series of quick wingbeats to regain altitude and reorient its heading. Tends to flock more prolifically outside of breeding season, but loose groups may still be observed in the late spring to midsummer near optimal feeding sites. Calls are high-pitched, burbling, and echoing.

MIGRATE? Yes.

NESTING: Cavity nester. Uses a natural tree hollow, former woodpecker nest, or manmade nest box (sometimes a martin house); this site is usually close to water. Inside, a loose bowl is formed of dried grasses and aquatic reeds. About 4 in. wide.

EGGS: Bright white. Length of ¾ in. Total of 3-7.

FEEDER BEHAVIOR: Does not visit feeders, but does use nest boxes.

COMPARE TO SIMILAR SPECIES: Iridescent, blue-green back is highly distinctive among the North American swallows. Furthermore, this species is much smaller than the Purple Martin, and has a white, rather than dark, underside.

DID YOU KNOW? A single Tree Swallow may catch over one million flying insects in a single year, especially if feeding its hatchling young for a portion of the summer. When extrapolated to account for localized populations of several thousand individuals, one can easily see the extent to which this species is dependent on insect populations—which have fallen in the Tree Swallow's typical habitats by as much as one-half in the past 50 years.

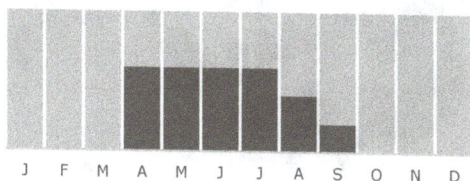

J F M A M J J A S O N D

① **WARBLING VIREO.** *Vireo gilvus.*

SIZE: 5 in.

HABITAT: Mature, open, usually deciduous woods—including some parks and suburbs. Often found near water.

WILD DIET: Mostly insects (e.g., caterpillars, beetles, butterflies) and spiders, but also fruits and berries (particularly before and during migration).

BEHAVIOR: A bird of the treetops, the vireo is more often seen than heard; however, for many suburbanites in older-growth neighborhoods, this may occur on a relatively frequent basis. This species hops along the branches, gleaning insects from the undersides of leaves, and occasionally resorts to hover-snatching for more elusive prey. Likely to aggressively guard nests from ovivorous, or egg-eating, predators. Like many vireos, males sing all throughout the day in spring and summer. Their song lasts a few seconds, consists of a series of up-and-down burbles and slurs, and is usually repeated after a few seconds' pause.

MIGRATE? Yes.

NESTING: Selects a location in a deciduous tree, with two intersecting branches forming part of the nest's rim. The nest is suspended from these anchor points, and takes the shape of a deep, hanging cup. Constructed with grasses and plant fibers, and tightly bound with spider silk. About 3 in. wide.

EGGS: White, with fine spotting. Length of ¾ in. Total of 2-4, with 1-2 broods.

FEEDER BEHAVIOR: Does not visit feeders.

COMPARE TO SIMILAR SPECIES: Very similar to other vireos, such as the Red-eyed and Philadelphia. The rounded, less boldly defined eyebrow distinguishes from Red-eyed, while the lack of bright yellow on the central underside differentiates from the Philadelphia. Warblers, such as the Tennessee, have a much thinner bill.

DID YOU KNOW? Vireos have lost well over half of their total populations in the past century, primarily due to the increasing usage of herbicides and pesticides.

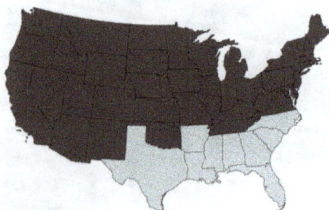

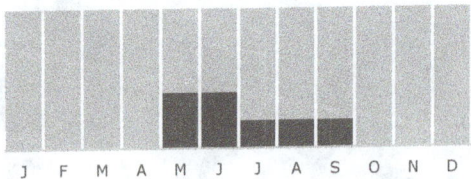

J F M A M J J A S O N D

Adults at top and bottom.

Adult above (Photo by Mdf / CC BY-SA / Cropped).

① LEAST FLYCATCHER. *Empidonax minimus.*

SIZE: 5 in.

HABITAT: Variety of woods, but usually open, mature woods with plenty of thickets.

WILD DIET: Insects. Sometimes, small fruits and berries in colder weather.

BEHAVIOR: Often on the move as it makes its way throughout the forest understory, flying between various perches (rarely returning directly to the same one) and hovering to grab insects from the air or vegetation. A feisty customer, this species is known to repeatedly chase away other birds from claimed breeding territories. Sings repeatedly during mating season, mostly in May.

MIGRATE? Yes.

NESTING: Semicolonial, with about 150 ft. separating individual nests of Least Flycatcher pairs. Selects a fork in a tree, in which a woven cup of grasses is constructed. About 2 ½ in. across.

EGGS: White. Length of ½ in. Total of 3-5.

FEEDER BEHAVIOR: Does not visit feeders.

COMPARE TO SIMILAR SPECIES: This species is a member of the *Empidonax* flycatchers, a group which also includes the Acadian, Alder, Willow, and Yellow-bellied Flycatchers. All are of similar coloration and size, and nearly indistinguishable by sight in the field. However, each has a very different song, and prefers a different habitat (though this can be less reliable during spring migration). The Least has a clipped, dry *che-beck* song; this lasts less than a quarter-second and may be repeated many times in relatively quick succession.

DID YOU KNOW? The smaller size and bold, white eye-ring of this species make it perhaps the most identifiable *Empidonax* flycatcher for novices, particularly during migration. In these months, many flycatchers are less discerning in their choice of habitat, thus nullifying what is normally a helpful differentiator. The *Empidonax* genus—of which the Least Flycatcher is a member—is host to a total of 11 North American species, many of which are nearly identical at a passing glance.

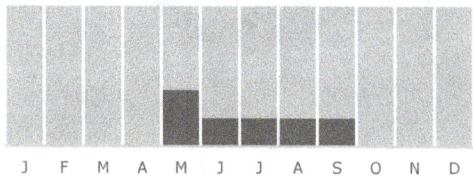

J F M A M J J A S O N D

② **COMMON REDPOLL.** *Acanthis flammea.*

SIZE: 5 in.

HABITAT: Coniferous forests. Sometimes (especially in irruptive winters), various open woods, overgrown fields, and suburbs.

WILD DIET: Small seeds (e.g., from cones of birch, spruce, pine). In summer, also consumes insects and spiders.

BEHAVIOR: Actively forages throughout the mid-canopy of mature, evergreen forests. In the far northern, arctic habitat where this circumpolar species frequently breeds, this may instead imply scrabbling over what little vegetation is present. Often present in flocks.

MIGRATE? Yes, but to varying degrees. In some winters, moves (or irrupts) southward in greater numbers when conifers have produced insufficient quantities of cones for winter feeding.

NESTING: In forks or crotches of trees. Messy cup of twigs, rootlets, and lichens. About 3-4 in. across.

EGGS: Light blue-green, with dark spotting. Length of ¾ in. Total of 3-7, sometimes with a second brood.

BIRD FEEDING TIPS

FEEDER DIET: Nyjer, black-oil and hulled sunflower seeds. **FEEDER TYPES:** Tubes, hoppers, platforms, ground. **FEEDER BEHAVIOR:** May irrupt once every two to three years, and numbers may still be insufficient to observe at feeders. Tends to flock and busily nibble at feed, similar to the behaviors of other species of finches.

COMPARE TO SIMILAR SPECIES: The similar Hoary Redpoll also may irrupt in winters with insufficient cone crops; however, the Hoary is a frostier white with less dark streaking, and has a conspicuous whitish patch on the lower back.

DID YOU KNOW? In the blustery depths of winter, some redpolls burrow into snowbanks for the night, staying warm by the insulation of their radiating body heat. Incredibly, these tunnels can reach up to two feet in length.

J F M A M J J A S O N D

Male at top, with red on throat, breast (Photo by Fyn Kynd / CC BY-SA / Cropped),
Female at bottom, with pale breast (Photo by Jean Burrell / CC BY-SA).

Adults at top and bottom.

(2) **BROWN CREEPER.** *Certhia americana.*

SIZE: 5 in.

HABITAT: Mature woods, both semi-open and dense. Often prefers conifers.

WILD DIET: Mostly insects and spiders; sometimes seeds in winter.

BEHAVIOR: The small stature and drab, well-camouflaged coloration of this tree-clinging species often make it difficult to spot—particularly when considering that it inhabits thicker, more mature tracts of woodland. However, this species' unique decurved bill and upward-spiraling hopping motion remain a distinct treat for any observer. The Brown Creeper frequently starts at the bottom of a tree, moving all the way to the top before repeating this pattern on a nearby tree. Additionally, the long, stiff tail acts like a brace when clinging to trees, similar to the behavior observed in woodpeckers, while its unusual bill is particularly adept at chiseling into the bark for insects. Its voice is typically thin, *seet*-like, and high-pitched.

MIGRATE? Partially.

NESTING: Selects a decaying opening in the tree bark, or a spot wedged between an extended bark slab and the trunk. Twigs, leaves, and grasses form a small cup nestled against the trunk. About 3-4 in. across.

EGGS: White, with reddish-brown spotting. Length of ½ in. Total of 4-7.

BIRD FEEDING TIPS

FEEDER DIET: Suet, peanut hearts, hulled sunflower seeds. **FEEDER TYPES:** Suet cages, tubes. **FEEDER BEHAVIOR:** Uncommon feeder visitor, and normally only takes suet.

COMPARE TO SIMILAR SPECIES: Most similar to the nuthatches, but upward movement along the trunk—as well as general appearance—is distinctive.

DID YOU KNOW? Referencing its especial climbing motion, a group of creepers is known as a spiral (e.g., a spiral of creepers).

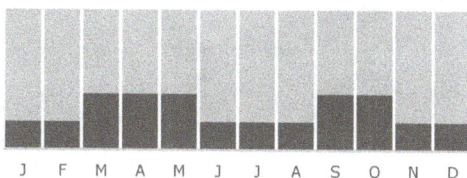

| J | F | M | A | M | J | J | A | S | O | N | D |

(5) **AMERICAN GOLDFINCH.** *Spinus tristis.*

SIZE: 5 in.

HABITAT: Overgrown fields and meadows, suburbs, and parks.

WILD DIET: Seeds (e.g., thistle, sunflower, dandelion, milkweed, alder).

BEHAVIOR: An active, social, and often highly visible finch, this species tends to hopscotch from plant to plant as it meticulously gleans the seeds which constitute the near entirety of its diet—a dietary trait known as *granivory*. Can be quite nimble as it clings to flowers and wispy clusters of foliage, as well as the links of metal fencing and other similar manmade objects, allowing this bird to reach a number of food sources that would be otherwise inaccessible. Sings with a high tone and cadence of *po-ta-to-chip*, and calls most frequently with a high, yanking duplet of whistles.

MIGRATE? Partially. Some individuals begin to move southward once temperatures dip below freezing, and particularly once they dip below zero.

NESTING: Usually in shrubbery or hedgerows, well elevated off the ground. Small cup woven of plant fibers, and lined with downy pollen. Anchored to branches with spider webbing. About 3 in. across.

EGGS: Off-white to light blue, with light spotting. Length of ¾ in. Total of 2-6, occasionally with a second brood.

BIRD FEEDING TIPS

FEEDER DIET: Nyjer, black-oil and hulled sunflower seeds, suet. **FEEDER TYPES:** Tubes, hoppers, platforms, ground. **FEEDER BEHAVIOR:** Very common at feeders, and tends to loiter in the same manner as House Finches. Molt can be gradually observed in early spring, transitioning from drab buff into bright yellow as it triumphantly enters its breeding season.

COMPARE TO SIMILAR SPECIES: Most similar to the smaller Lesser Goldfinch of the West and Southwest. Notable differences include the American's bright yellow (in breeding season) or pale back (nonbreeding), and orange bill (breeding). In addition, the Lesser rarely, if ever, occurs northeast of Missouri.

DID YOU KNOW? The American Goldfinch is the state bird of Iowa, New Jersey, and Washington.

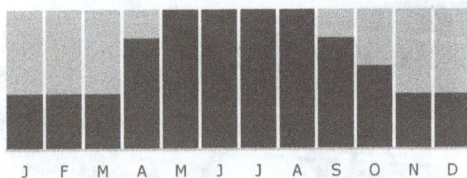

J F M A M J J A S O N D

Breeding female at top,
Breeding male at bottom left,
Nonbreeding adult at bottom right.

Adult male at top,
Adult female at bottom.

② **AMERICAN REDSTART.** *Setophaga ruticilla.*

SIZE: 5 in.

HABITAT: Large tracts of semi-open woods, often with thickets and situated near water.

WILD DIET: Mostly insects (e.g., moths, flies, caterpillars) and spiders. In early fall, occasionally consumes berries and seeds.

BEHAVIOR: This boldly colored warbler with the show-stopping, fan-shaped tail gracefully flits like a butterfly throughout the forest understory. Somewhat uniquely for warblers, it catches most of its insects aerially with flycatcher-like sallies, though it also gleans directly from branches. When approaching a brushy area, individuals will often open or fan their tails, flushing any nearby insects with a bright flash of color. Song is a series of burry *zeets* and effervescent whistles.

MIGRATE? Yes.

NESTING: Situated in a vertical fork of tree branches, usually adjacent to the trunk. A cup is manufactured to conform to the fork, and is well-woven with fine plant fibers, often bound with lichens or the nest combs of paper wasps. About 3 in. across.

EGGS: Off-white, with heavy reddish-brown speckling. Length of ¾ in. Total of 2-5.

FEEDER BEHAVIOR: Does not visit feeders.

COMPARE TO SIMILAR SPECIES: The male Blackburnian Warbler has orange that is limited to the head and throat, contrasting with the male American Redstart's fully black head. This species' coloration is also similar to that of the Baltimore Oriole, but note the redstart's much smaller size and differing foraging habits.

DID YOU KNOW? In Jamaica, this species is commonly nicknamed the "latrine bird" for its partiality for hanging around outdoor toilets and garbage dumps. These sites predictably host a king's ransom of flies, which the wintering redstarts gleefully devour.

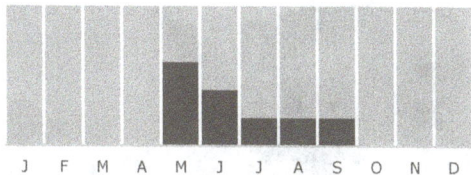

J F M A M J J A S O N D

② PINE SISKIN. *Spinus pinus*.

SIZE: 5 in.

HABITAT: Open woods, both coniferous and mixed. Also, suburbs and parks.

WILD DIET: Mostly seeds (e.g., from cones of conifers, dandelions, and wild grasses). Also, buds, stems, and insects and spiders.

BEHAVIOR: Often tucked away among the dense needles of conifers, darting from tree to tree as it pierces open seed pods, such as woody pine cones. May venture to ground level if fallen seeds or newfound sprouts appear. A somewhat opportunistic feeder, this species will nibble at leaves, stems, and even buds of garden vegetables if given the chance; it has also been known to eat the fallen pieces of seeds left by the foraging sessions of larger birds.

MIGRATE? To varying extents. In years with inadequate wild conifer cone yields, famished siskins move southward en masse.

NESTING: Concealed location in an outer fork of branches, often in a conifer. A slender-lipped bowl is woven of fine grasses, and lined with downy pollen or feathers. About 3-4 in. across.

EGGS: Light blue-green, with faint brown spotting. Length of ¾ in. Total of 3-5, occasionally with a second brood.

BIRD FEEDING TIPS

FEEDER DIET: Nyjer, black-oil and hulled sunflower seeds, suet. **FEEDER TYPES**: Tubes, hoppers, platforms, ground. **FEEDER BEHAVIOR**: May be somewhat common one year, and absent the next. Gregarious and genial. Attracted by extensive conifer plantings.

COMPARE TO SIMILAR SPECIES: May resemble a goldfinch, to whom this species is closely related, but the heavy streaking all across its body is very distinctive.

DID YOU KNOW? The Pine Siskin is well adapted to its typically northern environment. During winter nights, this species is able to survive temperatures as low as -100 °F by turning its fat-burning mechanisms into overdrive, and by converting large quantities of seeds stored in its throat pouch to thermal energy.

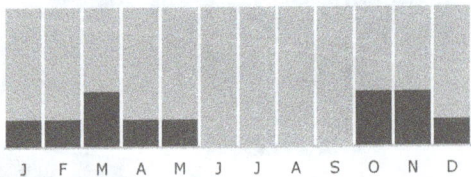

J F M A M J J A S O N D

Male at top (Notice heavy yellow on wings),
Female at bottom.

Adults at top and bottom.

① CHESTNUT-SIDED WARBLER.
Setophaga pensylvanica.

SIZE: 5 in.

HABITAT: Emerging patches of woods (i.e., with thickets and saplings).

WILD DIET: Mostly insects (e.g., caterpillars) and spiders.

BEHAVIOR: This prepossessing warbler is often found busily gleaning insects from the foliage of shrubs and small trees. Its habitat specialization signifies that individuals will often use a nesting habitat for five to ten years, before moving on to a more freshly emerging wooded habitat. Often characteristically holds its tail raised, as if ready to pounce on its next quarry. Its song is a rapid, almost murmured *pleased pleased pleased to MEETcha!*, which is most commonly heard in late spring and summer.

MIGRATE? Yes.

NESTING: Often located in forks of shrubs. A somewhat roughly hewn cup is woven of grasses and stems. About 3 in. across.

EGGS: Off-white to light blue-green, with brown speckling. Length of ¾ in. Total of 3-5.

FEEDER BEHAVIOR: Does not visit feeders.

COMPARE TO SIMILAR SPECIES: Bay-breasted Warbler may appear similar, but the Bay-breasted lacks a yellow crown and features a predominantly dark head.

DID YOU KNOW? Some warblers are known to hybridize, producing offspring with a mate of another warbler species. However, the Chestnut-sided Warbler was involved in perhaps the most unusual hybridization ever recorded, with an offspring of a male Chestnut-sided and a female Brewster's (which itself is a hybrid of the Golden-winged and Blue-winged Warblers) sighted and banded in 2018 in Roaring Spring, PA. This new hybrid, coined the Burket's Warbler after the landowner who originally discovered the individual, is the only three-species, triple hybrid observed in recent memory, and may be a sign that diminishing warbler populations are growing more desperate in their mating attempts.

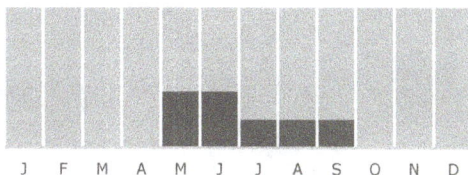

J F M A M J J A S O N D

② HOUSE WREN. *Troglodytes aedon*.

SIZE: 4 ¾ in.

HABITAT: Open woods, thickets, suburbs, parks, and gardens.

WILD DIET: Insects (e.g., caterpillars, ladybugs) and spiders (e.g., daddy longlegs).

BEHAVIOR: This species busily forages in the brushy understory of open woodland, searching for small, terrestrial insects and spiders. It is highly adaptable to various habitats, so long as they feature some brush or nearby thicket. Song is a burbling and rattling series of notes, which is typically only repeated throughout the spring and summer; in the spring, males frequently sing from elevated perches to attract mates, while females also sing during the nesting season to assert their dominance over the immediate area.

MIGRATE? Yes.

NESTING: Cavity nester. Selects a natural cavity, former woodpecker nest, or artificial substitute. A thin cup of twigs and grasses is lined with feathers. About 3-4 in. across.

EGGS: Off-white to light pink, with light speckling. Length of ¾ in. Total of 4-8, with 2 broods.

BIRD FEEDING TIPS

FEEDER DIET: Mealworms, suet. **FEEDER TYPES**: Platforms. **FEEDER BEHAVIOR**: Rare visitor. Most attracted by small platform cups filled with mealworms or bits of suet. Also, may use nest boxes and specially designed wren houses.

COMPARE TO SIMILAR SPECIES: Most similar to the regionally uncommon Winter Wren, which has dark belly streaking and is somewhat darker overall.

DID YOU KNOW? House Wrens are quite aggressive with regard to their nests. They have been known to fill the nests of nearby wrens with sticks, and even puncture their eggs. In addition, if a suitable nest cavity has already been taken, the female may displace the incumbent pair to take the location for herself.

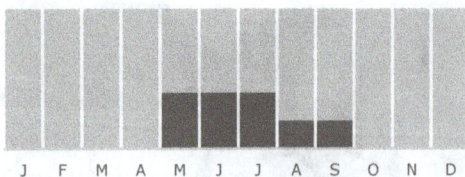

J F M A M J J A S O N D

Adults at top and bottom.

Adult male at top,
Adult female at bottom.

③ COMMON YELLOWTHROAT. *Geothlypis trichas.*

SIZE: 4 ¾ in.

HABITAT: Thickets, often near wetlands or edges of woods. May be observed in less densely thicketed areas during migration.

WILD DIET: Insects (e.g., beetles, ants, flies) and spiders.

BEHAVIOR: This species is often found scrambling about the low branches of damp thickets as it undertakes its daily foraging activities. The male's roguish mask is one of the most recognizable features on a North American warbler, and functions as a signal of masculine territoriality to its conspecifics. Song is a high, warbled series of *twiddly-twiddly-twiddly...*, which is very noticeable as males establish and maintain their breeding territories in late spring and summer.

MIGRATE? Yes.

NESTING: Near the ground, amid marshy vegetation. Nest is cup-shaped, and woven of dried reeds and stems. About 4 in. across.

EGGS: Off-white to light blue-green, with brown markings. Length of ¾ in. Total of 3-5, with 2 broods.

FEEDER BEHAVIOR: Rarely visits feeders, usually for suet.

COMPARE TO SIMILAR SPECIES: Male's black mask is fairly distinctive. Females are best distinguished by the combination of their yellow throat and breast, white belly, and olive back.

DID YOU KNOW? Of the billions of birds which migrate across the Gulf of Mexico each year, many fail to complete the parlous journey. As a result, tiger sharks—widely recognized for their wide-ranging eating habits, including the consumption of cans and license plates—have learned to congregate in certain sections of ocean where birds are most likely to fall, and Common Yellowthroats have been positively identified in the stomach contents of several analyzed tiger sharks.

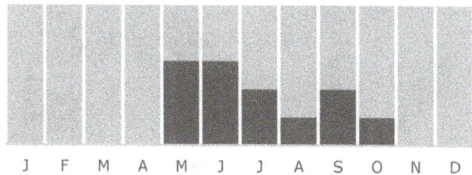

J F M A M J J A S O N D

① BLACK-AND-WHITE WARBLER. *Mniotilta varia.*

SIZE: 4 ¾ in.

HABITAT: Wide variety of woods, including well-wooded suburbs.

WILD DIET: Insects (e.g., caterpillars, ants, beetles) and spiders.

BEHAVIOR: This species is rather unique among the warblers, in that it frequently forages by clinging to tree bark. This nuthatch-esque behavior can be quite entertaining to watch, with individuals often hanging from branches, scraping at bark, and generally making acrobats of themselves. To suit these eclectic habits, this species' toes—particularly the hind toe—are longer than other warblers', which allows for a secure grip on vertical surfaces. Throughout the spring and early summer, Black-and-whites primarily consume caterpillars, which may be located on the undersides of difficult-to-reach branches. Song is a high, quick, and repeated *wheezy, wheezy, wheezy.*

MIGRATE? Yes.

NESTING: Selects a concealed location on the ground. A wide-rimmed nest cup is constructed with leaves and grasses. About 4-5 in. wide.

EGGS: Off-white, with reddish speckling. Length of ¾ in. Total of 4-5, occasionally with a second brood.

FEEDER BEHAVIOR: Does not visit feeders.

COMPARE TO SIMILAR SPECIES: Most similar to the Blackpoll Warbler, which is also black and white. However, while the Black-and-white features a boldly striped head, the Blackpoll instead has a plain, black cap and a broad, white cheek.

DID YOU KNOW? While a flock of warblers is commonly known as a bouquet, wrench, or confusion, the Black-and-white has its own collective noun; ergo, a flock is known as a *dichotomy* of Black-and-white Warblers—referencing the rather binary coloration of its plumage.

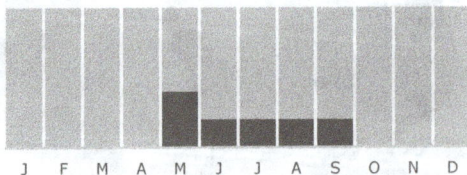

J F M A M J J A S O N D

Adult male at top (Note the black throat),
Adult female at bottom.

Adult male at top (Note the fully black throat),
Adult female at bottom.

① BLACK-THROATED GREEN WARBLER.
Setophaga virens.

SIZE: 4 ¾ in.

HABITAT: Mature, older-growth woods. During migration, also suburbs and parks.

WILD DIET: Mostly insects (e.g., caterpillars, flies) and spiders. Occasionally, berries.

BEHAVIOR: This species most commonly forages in the mid-level of trees, with short flights taking individuals from one feeding site to another. When foraging, this bird tends to either glean insects directly from branches, or undertake short aerial forays into swarms of flying insects. This species may also outcompete other warbler species for foraging space, forcing them to consider positions higher or lower in the trees. Song is a series of five to six buzzy *zee* notes, with a stressed, lower-pitch syllable (or two) in the back half of the tune.

MIGRATE? Yes.

NESTING: Selects a concealed location deep within the foliage of a tree. A compact cup is constructed with twigs and leaves. About 4 in. across.

EGGS: Off-white, with brown splotching. Length of ¾ in. Total of 3-5.

FEEDER BEHAVIOR: Does not visit feeders.

COMPARE TO SIMILAR SPECIES: The combination of black throat, yellow sides of face, and white belly are distinctive among regionally common warblers.

DID YOU KNOW? Like many warblers, the Black-throated Green Warbler is a highly productive vocalist. In fact, some have even recorded this species repeating its song as many as 500 times in a single hour.

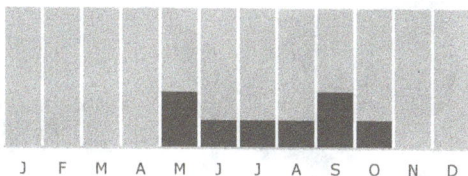

J F M A M J J A S O N D

③ **RED-BREASTED NUTHATCH.** *Sitta canadensis.*

SIZE: 4 ½ in.

HABITAT: Mature woods, both open and dense. Prefers conifers. In winter, may visit parks and suburbs with more regularity.

WILD DIET: Insects (e.g., ants, beetles) and spiders, seeds and nuts.

BEHAVIOR: The large, muscular claws of this species allow it to descend headfirst down trunks of trees as it forages, sometimes veering to one side or the other. Gleaned insects and seeds are increasingly stored in crannies and crevices of the bark as winter approaches. When flying between trees, an undulating flight pattern is observable—with brisk, sturdy flaps of the wings occasionally allowing the individual to regain altitude. Song and calls are a higher-pitched series of yanking guffaws than those of the White-breasted, its close genetic relative.

MIGRATE? Sometimes, and to varying degrees. When conifer seed crops are lower than usual, wide-scale irruptions of this species move southward in search of food.

NESTING: Cavity nester. Usually self-excavates, but may also use existing tree hollows or cavities. Inside, a rough bowl of bark and twigs is lined with feathers. About 4-5 in. across.

EGGS: White, with russet spotting. Length of ¾ in. Total of 3-8.

BIRD FEEDING TIPS

FEEDER DIET: Black-oil and hulled sunflower seeds, peanuts and peanut hearts, suet, mealworms, safflower seed. **FEEDER TYPES**: Tubes, hoppers, suet cages, platforms. **FEEDER BEHAVIOR**: Often observed making a series of quick visits, before flying away to hatch or store its haul. May associate with chickadees or titmice. May also use nest boxes.

COMPARE TO SIMILAR SPECIES: White-breasted Nuthatch is very similar, but lacks *a dark black eyeline* and orange-hued underside. Chickadees may also resemble this species, but note the differences in movement (i.e., rarely upside down).

DID YOU KNOW? Nuthatches are named for their proclivity for breaking apart, or hatching, large nuts in the hardened crevices of trees.

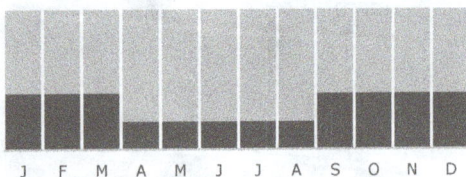

J F M A M J J A S O N D

Adult male at top (Note the darker cap and underside),
Adult female at bottom.

Adults at top and bottom.

② RUBY-CROWNED KINGLET. *Regulus calendula.*

SIZE: 4 in.

HABITAT: Breeds in mature, coniferous woods. During migration, often found in a variety of woods or thickets, including parks and suburbs.

WILD DIET: Insects (e.g., flies, ants) and spiders. Occasionally, fruits and seeds.

BEHAVIOR: This small bird has an enormously high metabolism, forcing it to forage actively all throughout the day. These caffeinated foraging habits often consist of hopping along branches, hovering near tips of branches or leaves, and sallying out into swarms of flying insects. Though less likely to flock with other kinglets during the breeding season—and often behaving quite territorially, with males flicking their rarely observed red head crests at rivals—this species often mixes with hordes of warblers and chickadees during migratory or wintering periods. Song is a distinctive mix of *seets*, chirps, trills, and slurs.

MIGRATE? Yes.

NESTING: Selects a location in a conifer. Nest is cup-shaped, and suspended from two or three branches, which are woven into the walls or rim of the nest. Constructed with a mix of grasses and feathers, and bound with spider silk. About 3-4 in. wide.

EGGS: Dull white. Length of ½ in. Total of 4-12.

FEEDER BEHAVIOR: Rarely visits feeders, usually for suet.

COMPARE TO SIMILAR SPECIES: Most similar to the closely related Golden-crowned Kinglet, which instead features a striped face and a visible golden-yellow head crest.

DID YOU KNOW? Relative to size, the kinglets lay the most eggs of any North American bird species. Just before laying, up to three-quarters of the female's weight may be comprised of her eggs alone—a truly remarkable feat.

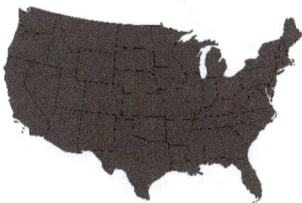

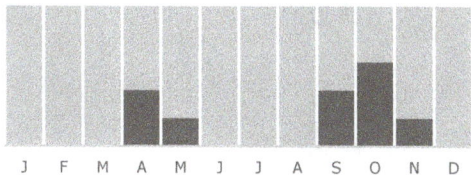

J F M A M J J A S O N D

① GOLDEN-CROWNED KINGLET.
Regulus satrapa.

SIZE: 3 ¾ in.

HABITAT: Breeds in coniferous woods. During migration and winter, may inhabit a variety of woods, including wooded parks and suburbs.

WILD DIET: Insects (e.g., flies, beetles, insect larvae) and spiders. Rarely, seeds.

BEHAVIOR: This highly active species is present in all levels of the forest, but most frequently in the canopy. Individuals forage by directly gleaning from branches, briefly hovering near clusters of leaves, and opportunistically flying into swarms of insects. The Golden-crowned is territorial in breeding season, but otherwise often associates in small groups with its fellow conspecifics or members of other species, such as chickadees, warblers, and titmice. Individuals may also be relatively tame around humans in some areas. This species' song is vaguely similar to the Ruby-crowned's, with a series of high, accelerating *seets* punctuated by several burbling warbles.

MIGRATE? Partially.

NESTING: Selects a high location in a conifer. Nest is hung from—or rests atop—a fork of branches, and is constructed with mosses and pieces of bark. Spider webbing is used for binding and anchoring. About 3 in. wide.

EGGS: Dull white. Length of ½ in. Total of 4-11, with 2 broods.

FEEDER BEHAVIOR: Does not visit feeders.

COMPARE TO SIMILAR SPECIES: Most similar to the closely related Ruby-crowned Kinglet, which lacks a striped face and a visible golden-yellow head crest.

DID YOU KNOW? The Golden-crowned Kinglet maintains an average internal body temperature of about 111 °F, which is 5-6 °F higher than that of most birds. Astonishingly, it is still able to survive long, cold winters at the northern extent of its breeding range: feasting on dormant caterpillars and insectile egg clusters by day, and roosting in sheltered crannies of trees by night.

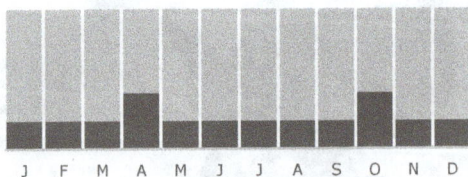

J F M A M J J A S O N D

Adults at top and bottom.

Adult male at top (Note: Red throat may appear blackish from a more severe angle),
Adult female at bottom.

③ RUBY-THROATED HUMMINGBIRD.
Archilochus colubris.

SIZE: 3 ¼ in.

HABITAT: Edges of woods, overgrown fields, gardens, suburbs.

WILD DIET: Nectar from flowers, flying insects. Also, sugar water from feeders.

BEHAVIOR: This high-revving species feeds on flower nectar all throughout the day, supplemented by a trickle of protein-rich, flying insects. Hovering and precise flight are facilitated by a wing mechanism unique to the hummingbird family: unlike other birds, which fold the wings on the upstroke, this species is able rotate its shoulders to provide propulsive thrust in all directions throughout a single wingbeat. Also like most hummingbirds, this species must feed every 15 minutes during the day to meet its exorbitant energy demands; during the nighttime, it compensates by entering a state of partial hibernation, known as *torpor.*

MIGRATE? Yes.

NESTING: Selects a location on top of a deciduous tree branch. Cup-shaped mound is formed of spider silk, pollen, and mosses. About 2 in. across.

EGGS: White. Length of ½ in. Total of 2. Raises 1-2 broods each year, occasionally 3.

BIRD FEEDING TIPS

FEEDER DIET: Sugar water. **FEEDER TYPES:** Nectar feeders. **FEEDER BEHAVIOR:** Perches or hovers at feeders. Males may act territorially near single-feeder setups.

COMPARE TO SIMILAR SPECIES: Males are quite distinctive across the region. Females of this species are very similar to female Black-chinned Hummingbirds, which normally summer in Texas and farther west; note that the female Ruby-throated's folded wingtips are straight and much slimmer.

DID YOU KNOW? Before migrating across the Gulf of Mexico, millions of hummingbirds gather along the coast, doubling their weights in the several days immediately preceding their departure. This ocean crossing is grueling, with up to one-quarter of all migrants failing to complete the perilous journey.

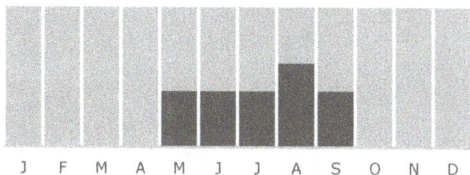

J F M A M J J A S O N D

INDEX OF SPECIES

SELECTED TITLES BY MARC PARNELL

The Birding Pro's Field Guides: City Series

Birds of Greater Chicago
Birds of Greater Cleveland, Pittsburgh, and Buffalo
Birds of Greater Dallas
Birds of Greater Houston
Birds of Greater New York City
Birds of Greater Washington, D.C.

The Birding Pro's Field Guides: State Series

Birds of Alabama
Birds of Arkansas
Birds of Connecticut
Birds of Delaware
Birds of Florida
Birds of Georgia
Birds of Iowa
Birds of Illinois
Birds of Indiana
Birds of Kansas
Birds of Kentucky
Birds of Louisiana
Birds of Massachusetts
Birds of Maryland
Birds of Michigan
Birds of Minnesota
Birds of Missouri

Birds of Mississippi
Birds of North Carolina
Birds of Nebraska
Birds of New Hampshire
Birds of New Jersey
Birds of New York
Birds of Ohio
Birds of Oklahoma
Birds of Pennsylvania
Birds of Rhode Island
Birds of South Carolina
Birds of Tennessee
Birds of Texas
Birds of Virginia
Birds of Vermont
Birds of Wisconsin
Birds of West Virginia

The Birding Pro's Field Guides: Province Series

Birds of Ontario

For a complete, updated list of titles, please visit our website at
www.thebirdingpro.com.

MARC PARNELL is a lifelong naturalist with a ceaseless passion for birding. He is currently the second most published ornithologist in the world by number of books in active print. Marc was born in Greenville, North Carolina, and presently resides in Cleveland, Ohio.

For press inquiries or event bookings, please contact the staff at Naturalist & Traveler Press, available at thebirdingpro.com.

If you enjoyed this field guide, please consider leaving a positive rating or review online at your place of purchase. As an independent publishing house, every bit of support is greatly appreciated.

Front Cover Photo: Yellow-rumped Warbler
Back Cover Photos: American Kestrel, White-breasted Nuthatch